THE COBBLESTONE FLOWERPOT

TROY DRAYTON

The Cobblestone Flowerpot
Copyright © 2017 by Troy Drayton

Printed in USA by Createspace (www.createspace.com)

About the Author

Troy was born in the Harlem neighborhood of New York City. Raised by his mother and grandmother, his upbringing was heavily impacted by the violence, impoverishment, and drug culture created in Harlem during the 1980's. From his circumstances, Troy gathered a sense of desperation that fueled his desire to provide a better life for his family. He used the adversity and hardships he faced as ambition to excel academically. Troy graduated from Binghamton University, which is held as a public Ivy, with a Bachelor of Arts degree in Economics. He currently works as an Analyst at Citigroup in Manhattan. During his time at the University, Troy took a number of philosophy classes for leisure. Intrigued by the power of philosophy and what it could do for minorities specifically, he made it a goal to make the subject more sought after and relatable to the average person. With this mission the general concept and framework for The Cobblestone Flowerpot was born.

Acknowledgements & Dedication

First, I would like to thank and acknowledge God. I direct all credit and honor to his guidance and favor. I was merely a vessel for this project and it would not have come into existence without his presence and position in my life.

Mom, thank you for always loving and supporting me unconditionally. Whether I wanted to be a writer or a rapper you provided your support and backing. It is this validation that makes me feel like I can be and accomplish anything in this world.

I would like to thank my closest friends - Danny, Nate, Derrick, Mic, Ron, Rell, Cj, Elijah, Jerrell, Gio, Uriah, Bri and the entire LB group as a whole. It was the events we've experienced together that have shaped and touched the perspective used to create this book.

To one of my most invaluable friends, Lyanne, thank you for listening and supporting this project when it was just an idea in my head.

Clarice, no words can express how pivotal you were to the creation of this project. It was your support that gave me the strength and motivation to finish the second half of this book. Thank you.

To the sights, residents, and business owners of Harlem, Brooklyn, Kenya, and Cuba (locations where this book was created) - Thank you for providing the inspiration I needed to complete this project.

Last, I would like to dedicate this book to my niece and sister. When in doubt please use this book to confirm - With God, anything is possible. Trust him with all your heart and he will forever be with you.

Table of Contents

Table of Contents

In Loving Memory of Nana Ama Atuah
July 17, 1993 – March 9, 2017

Foreword

When we teach literature to non-majors, one of the most important challenges that we encounter is to change the negative perception that many students have of common core classes. They come in intimidated by the amount of reading and writing that they have to do. When asked, "what kind of books do you usually read?" some might answer, "what teachers assign. Nothing else." It is our job to make literature speak to them in new ways so that hopefully in the future they would read more than we assign. The ultimate goal would be for these readings to de-familiarize the world around them and to push them to question their socialization. When Troy told me he wrote a book that was partially influenced by the texts that we analyzed in our class back in 2014, I was beyond happy. Here was a young man whose genuine interest in literature and philosophy remained with him even after graduation. He took that interest and immortalized it in words. – *Rania Said, Instructor and PhD Candidate at Binghamton University*

Preface

Throughout my life, I've had an affinity for helping people. As often as possible, I've tried to use my stories of overcoming adversity to inspire others. I believe this compelled my friends and individuals in general to ask for my insight and advice on the challenges they were facing. After years of similar deep conversations, I noticed a pattern in the areas of life they found most troubling - areas that routinely make us feel unfulfilled, inadequate, or stranded. Their fears were being incited by an ideology. An ideology of helplessness. I wrote this book with two purposes. First, to force readers to question what aspects of our lives are changeable. Second, to demonstrate how stoicism can help us approach the aspects of life we truly have no control over. In the end, I concluded this ideology is commonplace because it is perpetuated by contemporary thought.

The Cobblestone Flowerpot is a compendium of reflections written to provide an alternate perspective to contemporary thought. The ideas expressed within are modeled around the Stoic philosophy. Stoicism was derived from the idea of being stone-like. The philosophy teaches that emotions and impulses are the foundation of misfortune. It emphasizes that by living life using logic and reasoning we can elude pain and tragedy.

The Cobblestone Flowerpot displays that although idealistic in theory, the philosophy is partially impractical. These compositions demonstrate that by averting pain using this method you also avoid happiness. Ultimately, these writings will challenge what you've been taught your entire life. Do not just accept the ideas expressed in this book - question them, push back on them, and apply them as you feel fit.

Art makes us feel … love is art, hate is art, pain is art. Life becomes easier when we realize sometimes we are here to experience it and sometimes we are here to create it.

Troy Drayton

Chapter One: On Life

"Socrates: What if among the people in the previous dwelling place, the cave, [received] certain honors and commendations … for whomever most clearly catches sight of what passes by … What would the liberated prisoner now prefer?

Socrates: Do you think the one who had gotten out of the cave would still envy those within the cave and would want to compete with them who are esteemed and who have power? … Wouldn't he or she prefer to put up with absolutely anything else rather than associate with those opinions that hold in the cave and be that kind of human being?

Glaucon: I think that he would prefer to endure everything rather than be that kind of human"
 - **Dialogue from Plato's *Republic: "Allegory of the Cave"***

Some people remain in the dark because it is the only thing they know. Some people create excuses to justify living in the dark and therefore they are content with it. But others can't justify it. They crave the light but are afraid of the consequences. They wish to spread this light, but choose the comfort of conformity. They choose the comfort of conventionality. For many it is easier to follow the paths, traditions, and ideologies that have been set in place. However, the man who perfects a route is owed less praise than the man who creates one. Subsequently, if you have the power to inspire change, it is not a choice, it is a duty.

Plato examines this idea in his writing *The Allegory of the Cave*. He argues it's convenient for us to live in a system, a cave that controls our idea of what's acceptable. This system dictates what beauty is, what success is, what trendy is. It creates a hierarchy of people based on importance; those with wealth, degrees, and titles being at the apex. It places restrictions on what is "possible". Some people never think or question these things from an individual perspective. They just accept them. For others, it is all they think about. Plato argues it is easier to ignore what our mind is inherently telling us. He argues that some people never see the light outside of this system, others see the light and go running back to the cave. But some adjust to this light and spend their entire life trying to enlighten the cave.

Ultimately, your life will be defined by two overarching choices. You will build a life trying to be the person society tells you to be or you will tell society who you are. Plato concludes his writing by questioning if these two groups can coexist. He reaches the revelation that as long as society includes this group of thinkers there will always be conflict. Thinkers are a threat to the self-proclaimed power and structure of society. They are the outliers. They will face constant criticism and bear the burden of truth and knowledge.

The journey of life is less of a physical battle and more of an internal one. Our battles are with neither the controllable, nor the uncontrollable events we encounter, but rather the ideas we have developed about them. Our true battle is against the ideologies of entitlement and helplessness. Our problems are a result of our choices. They are created from our perspective on the situations we encounter. Our thought process and decision making is a greater hindrance to our journey than any outside force can ever be. Hence, the only difference between becoming and being is acknowledgement. When we master habitually making our attitude and choices ones that tend to our true selves we gain the ability to cherish life and everything it has to offer.

Chapter Two: On Purpose

"Your ambition should be to get as much life out of living as you possibly can, as much enjoyment, as much interest, as much experience, as much understanding. Not simply to be what is generally called a "success.""
- **Eleanor Roosevelt**

A single question shapes our lives. It comes in different forms and the urgency to answer it heightens with every passing day. Like a scratch we cannot reach, it is perpetually bothersome. Why am I here? What is my purpose? What am I here to do? The question becomes so pressing that we spend our entire lives trying to provide society with an one sentence answer; and that is the problem. Mitigating the depth and multilayered nature of this question is what makes it so challenging. The lack of attention and self-awareness used to approach this question presents us with our dilemma.

We have been taught since grade school this question should be easy to answer. Society's expectation is for us to have this answer by the end of high school. However, ponder what is being asked of us relative to our position in life at that point in time. Think about how immature, naive, and arrogant you are in high school. We lack life experience, career experience, relationship experience, travel experience, and above all independence. We have not experienced the adversity of adulthood and therefore we have a limited sense of self. As a result, we cannot determine what we want to do with ourselves because we have not yet become ourselves. Our lives are multidimensional. Our interests and purposes constantly change with daily interactions.

Attempt to grasp the absurdity of the question being posed. We never consider if the purpose of life is to just enjoy the journey. We don't perhaps because we believe this idea would make life meaningless; or possibly because we think so highly of ourselves that we can't accept humanity as just another group of living beings. Our intelligence is debatably our greatest strength and weakness. It is possible we are too intelligent to simply enjoy life. To put this in perspective think about when you travel to a foreign place. You do not ask yourself what is my purpose for being here. Your purpose is inextricably connected to your presence. You are there to explore, learn, and indulge in the experience. However, these things are perceived as minuscule and taken for granted in our everyday lives. We don't consider them a purpose and seldom do we view life in this manner. As an experience.

The fact is, we are not trying to answer the question, what is my purpose? We are trying to answer the question - what is my industrial place in society? Sigmund Freud discusses this idea in his writing

Civilization and its Discontents. He states, "in whatever way we define the concept of civilization, it is a certain fact that all the things with which we seek to protect ourselves against the threats that emanate from the sources of suffering are part of that very civilization." Freud is proclaiming that we value civilization because it makes us feel safe and in control of our lives, but at the same time it creates an obligation to be deemed as sufficient by others. As long as we continue to do this - to marginalize our lives to fit into a structure based on productivity, property, order, and belonging, we will fail to find our true purpose.

In the contemporary way we view this question, there is no answer. What you want to do and accomplish are your personal goals, they do not define why you are here. Too often these are viewed as synonymous. They are gravely different. We are here to experience life, to use the knowledge we gain to better ourselves and others. We are here to explore and diversify our mind so we can connect and understand the world we have been given. We are here to use our gifts and talents to contribute to the human experience. We are here to coexist with all living beings, to enjoy the universal principles of freedom, innovation, and happiness.

Chapter Three: On Happiness

"Enjoy the little things in life because one day you`ll look back and realize they were the big things."
- **Kurt Vonnegut**

Without the required effort, for every good day we have there will be an equal amount of bad days. This is because our perception of good and bad are interdependent. Our happiness is susceptible to this idea. In order to be happy, we must acknowledge the following I) Happiness is a never-ending pursuit. As humans, we grow and in the process, we develop new desires and goals. Our longing for fulfillment is inextinguishable. II) Happiness comes from within. Even on the days we perceive as bad days, happiness is present.

We can examine these ideas by measuring a person's happiness on a scale and analyzing their behavior over three days. On this scale a 10 represents the subject is at their happiest point, contrarily a 1 represents the subject is at their unhappiest point. If we measure a person's happiness on Monday and it ranks at 3, we can draw the conclusion this person is not very happy. If we measure this person's happiness again on Tuesday and it ranks an 8, we can draw the conclusion this person is notably happier than he was Monday. If we measure this person's happiness on the last day and it ranks a 6, from our experiment we would conclude this person is not as happy as they were on Tuesday, however they are significantly happier than they were Monday. If we had to report our findings we would confidently say overall this person is happy. This is not how the human mind functions. This person is highly likely to believe they are unhappy. The subject has experienced a higher level of happiness. They have quickly forgotten how unhappy they were Monday and they will now define how they feel and how they want to feel solely on their feelings from the day before. Although they are substantially happier than earlier in the week, they will perceive Wednesday as a bad day. It would take the subject a certain level of effort and consciousness to identify that in the larger context they are happy. Our life is essentially this three-day sequence looped continuously.

A key component to happiness is to not focus solely on the height of this scale but on its consistency. Based on our trial we proved a person who constantly thinks they are at a 6 will feel happier than someone who experiences high and low levels of happiness. This is why an unsuspectedly high number of people who acquire wealth, fame, and money feel unhappy. There happiness scale is now based on factors they cannot control. These factors and factors like these make our happiness scale volatile. Obtaining happiness in this way is unsustainable, these great highs set up great lows. Compare this to a poorer person. Their happiness will possibly rank at a lower number but their chart remains at or near this number consistently. Their happiness aligns with their appreciation for what they have. It comes from their interactions with their friends. It comes from having an opportunity to help their family. These things are more controllable. They do not waver as easily as materials and social status.

Epictetus, a slave turned Stoic Philosophy teacher believed we could place all of our encounters into two categories– things we can control and things we can't. In his writing *The Enchiridion* he states "Some things are in our control and others are not. Things in our control are opinion, pursuit, desire, aversion, and, in a word, whatever are our own actions. Things not in our control are body, property, reputation, public office, and, in one word, whatever are not our own actions. The things in our control are by nature free, unrestrained, un-hindered; but those not in our control are weak, slavish, re-strained, in the power of others. Remember, then, that if you suppose that things which are slavish by nature are also free, and that what belongs to others is your own, then you will be hindered. You will lament, you will be disturbed, and you will find fault both with gods and men. But if you suppose those things to be your own which are your own, and what belongs to others to be theirs, then no one will ever compel you or restrain you." Epictetus would argue we should place our happiness in the things we have control over. Yet, how feasible is this when so many things our out of our control?

We must create a happiness equilibrium. We are a culmination of our mind, body, and soul. When one component of our lives deteriorates, we need to be able to lean on the other components to maintain our happiness. We place most of our happiness in one or two faucets of our lives such as our jobs or significant others. When these things no longer exist, we have no source to pull our happiness from. Subconsciously we use these things to construct our identity. When they are no longer present we feel lost. To prevent this, we must distribute happiness into different aspects of our lives. Our mind is our source for learning and creativity. We can construct our identity on the things we are learning and creating. Our bodies are our physical selves. We should work on them and treat them with care. We can construct our identity based on our health and appearance. Our soul is our spiritual selves. We gain our divine sense of purpose and existence from our relationship with God. We can construct our identity on this relationship. When we look at our lives holistically it becomes clear we are in control of more than we think. We must diversify the areas we place our happiness, giving priority to the areas we can control when doing so.

We smile before we know how to walk. We laugh before we know how to read or write. We have our seemingly most fulfilling and happiest days before we enter adulthood. We are born happy. Happiness is and will always be within us. As we get older and are taught the expectations of society, we lose sight of this.

Our definition of happiness becomes more peculiar. Anxiety and outside pressure build as we try to achieve something that we already have. We begin to base our happiness on external and superficial factors. We link our joy to the pursuit of obtaining wealth, materials, relationships, careers, titles, and accolades. Consequently, our happiness is based on how we believe we are perceived by others. The problem with defining happiness in this sense is its perpetuity. A renewing sense of purpose can be a rewarding aspect of happiness, but only when our new desires are being conceived from a true notion of what we want. If not, we are creating a growing void in our soul that is impossible to fill.

We are seeking an earthly validation that will never be satisfied. No matter how much we acquire we will only be satisfied momentarily before our desire for this validation re-presents itself. This will become an endless cycle of subconsciously setting goals not for ourselves but for others.

By definition - to be content is to be in a state of peaceful happiness. Yet, we are raised to strive for the exact opposite – to never be content. We are hardwired to place renewing expectations on every aspect of our lives. Therefore, we must achieve contentment in a different form – we must be content with the drive, attitude, and work ethic we extend toward these expectations and not the outcome itself.

Chapter Four: On Love & Relationships

"What else is love but understanding and rejoicing in the fact that another person lives, acts, and experiences otherwise than we do?"
- **Friedrich Nietzsche**

To be in a healthy relationship, a person must first understand what a relationship is. It is commonplace to romanticize about the idea of having a significant other, but challenging to conceptualize how difficult and abnormal this task is. A relationship is two separate human beings with different life experiences, morals, perspectives, goals, and values trying to mend together and become one unit. No matter how closely these attributes align they will never be an exact match. As a result, it is inevitable in any union of this type, there will be recurring friction.

Plato alludes to this friction in his writing *The Symposium*. He argues we are magnetized to our partner's differences because "true love is admiration." Plato believes we become most attached to the people who have qualities and attributes we ourselves lack and we admire them because of these differences. They become the missing piece to our puzzle and make us feel whole. Their differences are the key to diversifying our perspective and unlocking our true potential. Plato would argue to be in a relationship we must accept our partners will change us. Consequently, each partner must be dedicated to learning from the other and accepting their differences are a strength in their relationship and not a weakness.

Unfortunately, this friction is often the demise of a relationship. It creates doubt, insecurity, and most dangerous of all, the presence of the imagination or the rising question of "what if?" Curiosity, pride, vanity, lust, and similar superficial attributes are often the subtle executioners of relationships. It is the notion that this friction is a sign of a failing bond that begins to unravel them. The truth is within this friction lies the beauty of the relationship. It encompasses the idea that two people with the improbable chance of meeting have decided to constantly work, relearn, and adapt to each other no matter how hard this task becomes. Despite the temptation of outside forces, or disruptive nature of internal ones, two people have found something worth dedicating their lives to.

The success of a relationship is contingent on the two parties being able to accept the following statements as true. I) To be in a healthy relationship with another person you must first have a healthy relationship with yourself. II) A healthy relationship is a job. It requires constant work and rightfully so it must be governed by principles.

Among these principles are the three C's of a healthy relationship. Communication, Compassion, and Compromise. Communication is the imperative binding force in a relationship. Without communication, any union will lack a solid foundation. Communication creates transparency. It eliminates assumptions, misunderstanding and insecurities. It builds trust. With communication and transparency no outside force can infiltrate the two parties. Ultimately, it grants protection and the ability to build on both things the parties like and dislike about the relationship.

Next is compromise. It is human nature to want to satisfy our personal desires. We view life through a lens. This lens is based on our perspective. We define our daily interactions through our perspective. Our morals and ideas of what is right and wrong, acceptable and unacceptable are founded upon it. Therefore, it takes energy and consciousness to focus on how our actions and desires can counteract and affect others. Compromise is undeniably one of the most undermined attributes in a relationship. It is the unsung saving grace of unions. In a relationship, you must occasionally and reasonably yield your wants and desires for your partner. You must ask how your decisions and actions will make them feel.

The last principle is compassion. To be human is to be flawed. Error is what keeps us from being machines.

We make mistakes. Compassion is what allows us to forgive. It is essential for all humans to have compassion. This is only amplified with your partner. There will undoubtedly be times when we don't meet each other's expectations. The answer is not to give up. Just like in academia we progressively learn from our mistakes. The end goal is not to get a perfect score on every test, although that is ideal it is also impractical. The ultimate goal is to build your knowledge so that you have fully grasped all the material needed to do well on the final test. In the case of a relationship this exam is learning how to love, protect, and coexist with your partner. Mistakes prepare both partners for this task.

If the above is true it invokes a logical question. How do we know when to let go? Friedrich Nietzsche makes an argument that the answer is encompassed in our ability to hold conversations. In his writing, *Human, All Too Human,* He states "When entering into a marriage one ought to ask oneself: do you believe you are going to enjoy talking with this woman up into your old age? Everything else in marriage is transitory, but most of the time you are together will be devoted to conversation." If you are still able to engage in conversations with your partner that make you laugh, make you think, inspire you and make you forget the world consists of more than yourselves, there is something there worth fighting for. Although seemingly simplistic, this kind of conversation is impossible to conjure when the damage in the relationship is irreversible.

Love is unconditional. Love is difficult. Love is caressing a person's flaws, fondling a person's imperfections, staring at all the ugliness the world has instilled within them and accepting they still deserve your love. Our desire to want a life partner is one of our natural instincts. We yearn for companionship. With a spouse, we get much more. For this reason, barring infidelity or any form of abuse, we should invest the necessary time and energy in building a healthy union.

Chapter Five: On Profit Based Education

"I have never let my schooling interfere with my education."
- Mark Twain

Formal schooling is an indispensable component of any society. However, it should not be used as the sole indicator of a person's mental capacity. Intelligence is a measure of the information we obtain, our ability to retain that information & how effectively we are able to apply that information. In theory, school systems provide a systematic way to deliver and record the metrics of the first point. It does not address the second or third. It cannot measure how long a person retains information or how effectively they will be able to apply it in real world scenarios.

Formal schooling is not an exclusive means to education. School is an institution, which has historically been reserved for the bourgeoisie and elitist. Traditionally the academy has been an institution used to prepare members of these privileged classes for occupations in art, literature, medicine, and science. Due to advancements in educational rights, formal schooling is now obtainable across social classes in most modern societies. Yet, the system is still most advantageous to its initial attendees. Profit based education prevents the school system from being an equalizing pillar in society. It allows the remnants of privilege and separation to continue. As long as this structure remains in place there will be little or no mobility for the lower class as a whole.

Diplomas and formal education are a gateway to high earning jobs. Our intellectual capabilities are additionally judged based on the school we obtain these degrees from. This process is flawed because the quality of profit based vs. universal education prior to higher learning varies. This creates two fundamental problems. I) The range of career paths are limited for those who receive a poor quality of education. II) All students will eventually reach a standardized point regardless of their profit based or universal education status. This presents a challenge for students who received a low level of education. They bear the burden to not only compete against better prepared students for admission but also adjust to a higher level and pace of learning if accepted.

Essentially having separate education systems implements limitations that are favorable to a caste system. Just because these two roads eventually merge does not mean we can ignore their starting points. Although both groups receive an education the careers they are deemed qualified and embark on will also be split into two groups. In both cases our education systems are built to prepare students to specialize in a field as oppose to prepare them for the real world. An emphasis is placed on test preparation as opposed to real world application. Courses are built around theory and not practical interaction. At the end of our long road through academia we have gained a great deal of hypothetical knowledge for situations we are unlikely to come in contact with. We are merely an unshaped ball of clay ready to be molded and used by the highest bidder.

Outside of media there is no better place to control the masses than school. For this reason, self-education is an imperative supplement to any formal schooling. In the era of information, self-education should be our most coveted priority. It allows us to focus on topics that matter to us. This leads to self-discovery and the ability to utilize our knowledge in a way we deem fit.

We can use German philosopher Immanuel Kant's concept of the Categorical Imperative to distinguish the primary difference between school and education. The Categorical Imperative is a moral principle derived to help us judge how we treat others. It states, "treat humanity, weather in your own person or in the person of another as an end in itself and not merely a means." Things we use as means to an end are only connecting pieces. Their value is contingent on their ability to grant our goal. Hence if this goal is eventually deemed as superficial, flawed, impure or simply unachievable, the value of the means taken to obtain it is questionable. Things we deem as ends in themselves are intrinsically valuable. Once we obtain them we are fulfilled and have the option to further their use. School is a means to an end, it is an institute utilized to gain a degree and furthermore a job. Education is an end in itself. It is satisfying. It is not dependent on the validation of a degree. Consequently, it is what we use to mold and shape ourselves. In order to forge our own path independent of the agenda of others we must sharpen our minds. The piece of paper we call a diploma is a tool, but our mind is the key that ultimately opens the door.

Chapter Six: On Principles

"He hadn't cut corners though or played all the angles. He was diligent and honest, no matter what it cost him. He had led his life according to principles that demanded a different kind of toughness, principles that promised a higher form of power. I would follow his example, my mother decided. I had no choice. It was in the genes."
- **Barack Obama describing his father in his Autobiography** *Dreams from my Father*

There is no coin so precious that it is worth a clear conscious and few fates worse than the inability to look at oneself in the mirror. Two factors distinguish humanity from other living beings, our intelligence and moral inclination. The ability to create boundaries and limits separates us from the animal world. We construct our lives based on an ethical code, creating principles that govern our actions. These principles exhibit what we stand for. They are connected to our integrity and honor, which above all superficial virtues and material objects, establishes the foundation of how we value our existence. For this reason, our principles are an integral part of our identity.

When we compromise them we lose a piece of ourselves. Our principles materialize into the earthly representation of our soul. They are personified through the way we treat others, what we are willing to tolerate and the issues we defend. Ultimately, they display what lies beneath the flesh, muscles, and bones; they display who we are at our core. Like attempting to build on sinking soil, all efforts made to advance ourselves by means that sacrifice our principles will manifest failed results. The allure of social gratification and/or fear of public condemnation forces us to abandon our principles. Our yearning for social acknowledgement challenges our ability to maintain our self-security. It is within this internal battle we lose or establish ourselves.

Plato examines this idea in his text *Crito*. The dialogue is set in Socrates's prison cell as he awaits his death. Socrates is refusing to accept the guaranteed escape Crito has prepared for him. He is attempting to convince Crito why he should not leave. Socrates escaping is a matter of honoring or dishonoring his principles. They are connected to the Athenian laws in which he helped create. Socrates's argument rests on this question – What quality of life will remain if he sacrifices his principles to elude death? Crito believes he is required to assist Socrates in escaping because the city will think poorly of him if he does not. Crito is an individual of high status and a well-known friend of Socrates. He believes if he does not compromise the principles he shares with Socrates it will reflect negatively on how he is publicly perceived. Socrates disputes this reasoning stating "Why, my dear Crito, should we care about the opinion of many? Good men, and they are the only persons who are worth considering, will think of these things as truly as they happened." Socrates is arguing that the opinion of others should be disregarded. Only the opinion of "good men", who will consciously and circumstantially view these events matter. It is these good men who understand the importance of honoring our principles.

Additionally, Socrates alludes to the idea that our principles are not bendable. To justify our actions, we try to measure how much we can compromise them. But, this is not how it works. Embedded in our principles is our notion of what is right or wrong. We must pick one, there is no in between. We cannot choose to honor them when they are advantageous but discard them in the presence of an award.

Seldom do we abandon our principles in an attempt to convince ourselves of our capabilities. We want to meet the expectations of others. We know we can achieve the same results, but we are afraid of how we will be viewed if we do not. In all applicable scenarios, the root of dishonoring our principles is a result of our desire for social validation and for the same reason it is detrimental to our inner prosperity. No one can lay a foundation other than the one already laid. If anyone builds on this foundation using gold, silver, precious stones, wood, hay, or straw, his workmanship will be evident, because the day will bring it to light. It will be revealed with fire, and the fire will prove the quality of each man's work. What has a man who has gained the world at the cost of his soul truly obtained?

In the end our earthly possessions have little value. At our funerals, there will be few references made on how much money and how many titles we acquired. At that moment, these things don't mean much. The people there don't mourn these things. They mourn how you treated them, the promises you kept, the person you were and the role you played in their lives. Upholding our principles requires discipline but grants us peace. Our principles are invaluable. Ultimately it is imperative we keep, practice, and protect our principles no matter the perceived cost. The consequence of abandoning our principles are far greater than any social consequence or reward.

Chapter Seven: On Ownership

"Rather go to bed without dinner than to rise in debt."
- Benjamin Franklin

The foundation of our nation's [United States] economy is debt. The idea of credit has become so commonplace we give little thought to its irrationality. It has become so normalized we perceive credit as being more valuable than tangible money. We place more value on credit cards than we place on debit cards. We lease and rent products instead of owning them. Our housing, automotive and education systems are structured around it. It has become such an imperative faucet of our lives; the fore mentioned sectors are virtually unobtainable without it. We are obsessed with credit. Why? Credit heightens our financial freedom. In a very practical sense if we do not have enough money for an object we cannot afford it. Credit nullifies this fundamental truth. It creates the notion we have more money than our tangible assets reflect. We have become accustomed to instant solutions. Credit satisfies our desire to obtain materials immediately.

When credit is not used as an investment tool, it is an extraneous component of society. It exists primarily as an exploitive financial device. I) As long as credit lines exist people who possess or have access to large amounts of money can capitalize off those who do not. II) Credit facilitates product pricing. It allows companies to overprice products and still target demographics who without credit could not afford it. III) Credit creates a scoring system that marginalizes individuals.

Both governments and corporations gain economically from the increase in spending perpetuated from credit. It's most impactful ramification is it mitigates the importance of ownership. We have become comfortable with the idea of borrowing. Credit creates the feeling that we are not spending our own money. Contrarily it increases our residual outflow of money. At the end of every credit cycle we pay the borrowed amount back with interest. This has a negative impact on our ability to save. Low levels of saving along with low levels of income and investment are conducive to what is referred to in economics as the poverty trap. The lack of these factors along with other forms of capital makes it difficult to obtain sustainable economic growth. As a result, there is a cycle of generations who cannot reach the next financial bracket. This occurs on both a macro level effecting developing countries; as well as a micro level effecting "developing communities." Credit administered that is not used for investment in some form of capital is detrimental to escaping this poverty trap.

The implications of the credit score system is twofold. I) It implicitly makes credit mandatory. The scoring system is used as a qualifying tool when assessing applicants. The problem is the level of emphasis placed on the credit score. The credit score is deemed equally if not more important than the other requirements. This means an individual can provide proof they have the satisfactory income or a sufficient amount saved to acquire a product, but if they do not have the credit score they will still be denied. Consequently, individuals must pursue and maintain credit as a means to function in society. II) The credit score does not substantially prove anything. It has little real world value. A person deciding to pay a student loan or a cell phone bill late is a very different decision than if the same person will or will not pay their rent. The elasticity of these factors vary greatly. As a result, it is like comparing two different metric units. A credit score used to examine applicants for housing should be composed of credit information based on their housing history. If not, it is comparing apples to oranges.

The availability of credit effects many aspects of society. When used properly it has the capacity to be a vehicle for social mobility. Yet it is primarily used as a means to continuously borrow instead of own. Ownership is critical component of our financial health. Owning our assets lessens monthly spending. Funds that would be spent on these bills can be saved or invested. By owning our assets, we have something to give to our next generation. Owning our businesses enables us to create wealth and allocate it amongst family and friends. Owning our property allows upcoming generations to inherit fixed assets. They can now save and invest more than the previous generation. Slowly there will be an accumulation of wealth as more money begins to come in than money that is going out. A cultivator's true reward is not seen today. Their garden will continue to bear fruit after they are gone. Their children will always have a trade; and if the demand for fruit falls, they will sell wine.

Chapter Eight: On Self-Love

"Most of the shadows of this life are caused by standing in one's own sunshine."
- **Ralph Waldo Emerson**

• Sam Bowie was selected as the No. 2 pick in the 1984 NBA Draft, one spot ahead of Michael Jordan.

• Since the inception of the NFL draft through 2016, eighty-one players have been drafted first overall. Only twelve have been inducted into the Pro Football Hall of Fame. Only five have been selected the NFL Rookie of the Year.

• Baseball Hall of Famer Mike Piazza, one of the greatest catchers in the history of the sport was drafted in the 62nd round (Pick # 1,390).

• 5 time NFL champion Tom Brady was drafted by the New England Patriots with the overall 199th pick.

Professional teams allocate millions of dollars to develop recruitment departments and hire professional scouters. They watch players for years. They analyze their numbers. They identify their strengths and weaknesses. They monitor their health and abilities. Yet they still make the wrong choice. These inaccurate picks are not because they miscalculated the potential of the other options but because they had a premeditated idea of what traits were conducive to their team's success. The prioritizing process begins prior to the decision-making process. Someone's inability to see our worth is not a representation of our value. It is merely a reflection of what traits they deem important.

We undermine the complexity of the human perspective. Our outlook is not something we develop overnight. It is the culmination of the experiences we have observed throughout our lifetime. It is the reason we place emphasis on some values as opposed to others. It is ingrained in our thought process and reflected in our decision making. It is a common misconception that we can change the perspective of others. We cannot. No matter how hard we try, our effort will be futile. A person's perspective will only change with a self-conscious choice or through experience. Our perspectives are most often changed through adversity or misfortune. Yet we long for others to see what makes us special. So much so we repeatedly attempt to display these attributes in various forms. What we are actually asking, is for this person to see what we find special about ourselves. We want them to acknowledge what we deem makes us qualified, unique, and different. But the truth is as greatly as we value our attributes they may be completely meaningless to others.

The importance of these values is not held to a universal standard. They vary depending on a person's perspective. Loyalty maybe important to one person, but not equally important to someone else. It is the disconnect in the importance we place on values that leads us to the classic question. Why am I not good enough? We are good enough. As people grow their perspectives grow. They begin to place emphasis on values they once deemed as unimportant. Essentially, we have different individuals at different stages of their lives interacting with each other and defining themselves by each other's perspective. This is problematic because we can meet someone who is inexperienced. But we will adjust how we view ourselves based on their perception. If you show a person you are intellectual, but they place a greater importance on physical traits, it will be easy for them to disregard you. Not because you are not an intellectual or because this is not an important trait, but because they have not had enough experience to value this trait yet. Unfortunately, distinguishing which qualities a person values is not easy. It cannot be displayed through words, only action.

We must first appreciate the qualities we possess. We will continuously encounter people who undervalue our attributes. It is not our job to persuade them. Their perspective does not lessen the things we find special about ourselves. As Deepak Chopra states "[We] are totally independent of the good or bad opinion of others."

Nothing anyone does is a result of our being. It is merely a reflection of the place they are at in their lives. Too often we question what we have done to induce unfavorable responses from the people we care about, but we disregard they had many options when choosing their response. i.e.) When someone ignores us we ponder what we did, or why we are not worth a response. There are infinite possible answers to this question, all which only the ignorer can answer. The more important question we should ask is why did this person believe among all their options the response to ignore us was acceptable let alone, the best choice. When we ask this question we quickly find a substantial answer. We see how deeply a crack can run through one's flowerpot.

The same idea is applicable in situations of infidelity, and betrayal. Situations like these seem extremely personal, but have very little to do with the person being subjected to them. The acts of this person will usually happen again to the next person in this position. Consequently, we should practice the advice author Don Miguel Ruiz offers in his writing *The Four Agreements*. He states "Whatever happens around you. Don't take it personally. Nothing other people do is because of you. It is because of themselves." But how practical is this? We live in a social world and must interact with others. How can the responses we receive not be a direct reflection of our interactions? We can add clarity to Ruiz's assertion by borrowing insight from an

African proverb commonly referred to as *The Fable of the Lion and the Gazelle* – "Every morning in Africa, a gazelle wakes up, it knows it must outrun the fastest lion or it will be killed. Every morning in Africa, a lion wakes up. It knows it must run faster than the slowest gazelle, or it will starve. It doesn't matter whether you're the lion or a gazelle-when the sun comes up, you'd better be running."

Although poetic in nature, the fable bears a substantial teaching point – At first glance, it's easy to judge others by their actions towards us. We must ask ourselves how differently would we view these actions if we took the time to examine how they are linked to the person's own sense of survival or sense of self? In other words, it's hard to see how much sense these actions make to the lion unless we were a lion ourselves. The difference between right & wrong is often found in the skipped moment that should have been used to gauge perspective... Don't skip that moment. When we do we deprive others of their wholeness, and we place underserving culpability on ourselves.

In his writing, *On the shortness of life*, Seneca promotes the importance of being cognizant when deciding the people, we accept in our lives. He states, "We must be especially careful in choosing people and deciding whether they are worth devoting a part of our lives to them, whether the sacrifice of our time makes a difference to them." Nothing in life – no material object, idea, or physical being possesses any inherent value or meaning. We allocate meaning to everything. How we value and view ourselves is the most instrumental factor in who and what we decide to distribute it to. If you find yourself having to constantly prove your worth to someone, discard them. Whisper to them "You are only flesh, my mind has conjured the idea you were important, and now I will take this precious gift back."

We are responsible for loving the attributes we possess regardless of how they are deemed by others. Self-validation is the only validation worth seeking. Our perspective is the only one we control. Loving ourselves gives us freedom. It grants us the confidence needed to make the world adjust to us. Self-love effects every aspect of our lives. It attracts the proper energy and people. When we determine our worth we create a standard for ourselves. Our willingness to tolerate anything under this standard becomes unimaginable. Not settling becomes a habit. Our careers, aspirations, and personal relationships must align with this standard or they will be discarded. Time becomes our most cherished possession and we become conscious and selective of how we allocate it.

We should cherish both our physical and intangible attributes. They define who we are. They were created through unique circumstances. Our imperfections tell our story. Our scars prove we were here. We are all someone's missing piece. There is no need to change ourselves to fit someone else's puzzle. We must learn to value ourselves so deeply we find it laborious to recognize the existence of those who don't. It should be an exhausting task to entertain those who do not properly value what we have to offer.

In the end, we determine our self-worth. We were not created to be accepted by everyone. The greatest gift we can give to ourselves is the acknowledgement that we deserve to be loved. Until we conquer self-love, we will not be able to properly give or receive any other form of love.

Chapter Nine: On Captivity

"I freed a thousand slaves I could have freed a thousand more if only they knew they were slaves."
- Harriet Tubman

The Conventional 9-5 Work Schedule:
7am-6pm: 11 hours
11 hours preparing for, traveling to, at or returning from work.
11 x 5: 55 hours per week spent on something work related.
8 x 5: 40 hours per week sleeping.
95 hours in a 5-day week is spent on something work related or sleeping.
24 x 5= 120 hours in a 5-day week.
95/120= Approximately 80% of a 5-day week is spent on something work related or sleeping.

      This is a snapshot of our lives. We disproportionally engage in work. Almost every day we trade hours of our lives for money; undermining the opportunity cost of every hour we spend working. For some this is idealistic. We have been taught that the pursuit of money is among the most important objectives of life. For others, this is absurdity. No matter our stance we must oblige. There is no alternative to this system. In order to live we must be a part of it. When we wake up, no matter how badly we want to return to bed, we have to go to work. In this instance, the fallacy of choice reveals itself.

Albert Camus sheds light on this plight in his philosophical essay *The Myth of Sisyphus*. Sisyphus was a figure in Greek Mythology who was forced to carry a boulder to the top of a mountain and watch it roll down just to do this task repetitively for eternity. Camus argues that Sisyphus punishment is a metaphor for the plight of the working man. His punishment is not as much the weight of the boulder but the repetition of engaging in an unfulfilling task every day to no end. At the conclusion of the essay Sisyphus is no longer sure whether it is him or the boulder that is made of stone. His premise can be summed up by this quote from the essay – "The workman of today works every day in his life at the same tasks, and this fate is no less absurd. But it is tragic only at the rare moments when it becomes conscious."

This is not freedom. It is slavery for profit. Paradoxical in a literal sense, but not from a moral standpoint. Relieve yourself of one misconception - this is not how life has to be; this is a system that has been chosen. This system perpetuates the mass selling of labor so few men can profit greatly, so these few men can have true freedom. From our labor, they gain the ability to create their own schedule - wake up when they want, spend their days with their family and answer to no one. This system promotes one goal, self-advancement. The majority of society wakes up every day to push themselves one step higher on a non-existent ladder. Even if it means belittling, lying, or sabotaging others in the process. The result is a society that has become accustom to mud-slinging. A society that points fingers first and searches for solutions after. A society absent of accountability and growth.

We have the intelligence to develop a system that is conducive to freeing our time and maximizing our happiness. A system that is not based on money dictating our livelihood. Implementing standardized salaries across occupations would incentivize individuals to choose careers they are passionate about opposed to ones with higher wages. Shortening the work week would give individuals more time to do the things they love outside of work. Administering a combination of these changes could create a system that increases society's utility as a whole. But this is not an appealing change for the people who are in positions to spearhead it. It would destroy the hierarchy set in place. The disparity in pay grades and life styles would shorten. For the people who buy our labor this is a nightmare. They build their fortune on this labor, but allocate just enough of their gained wealth to keep their workers content.

If philosophy is the vehicle that guides humanity, economics is the engine. It is the driving force that affects our value system; and capitalism is an incapacitating oil leak. In his writings, Philosopher and Economist Karl Marx discusses in depth the relationship between philosophy and economics. His work is most often associated with the development of communism, but should be cited for its efficiency in identifying the perils of capitalism. Marx realized Capitalism makes us competitive, possessive, complacent, and unpassionate. It influences our decisions by adding monetary value to things that otherwise would have little meaning such as materials, jobs, and houses. It focuses on specialization, forcing us to follow one path which directly clashes with our inherent multi-faceted composition. It demonizes unemployment, and unnormalizes our desire for leisure. Marx's Communist Manifesto was less of a supporting document for communism than an urgent cry for emancipation. It was an abolitionist handbook for humanity.

It should be hard for anyone to accept the idea they were born to spend such an immense portion of their lives working. Our earned money is taxed both when we receive it and when we spend it. Add this to our monthly bills and it becomes evident the cost to live in this system exceeds the weight of Sisyphus's boulder.

Life should not feel like a rollercoaster. Our time on this planet is finite. Everyday should feel important. Instead of waiting for two days of freedom, we should feel good and look forward to each one. This becomes a significantly less difficult task when we learn to live our life based on purpose and passion as opposed to money and escapes. When Nelson Mandela reflected on the twenty-seven years of his life he spent imprisoned, the South African president said "To go to prison because of your convictions and be prepared to suffer for what you believe in, is something worthwhile. It is an achievement for a man to do his duty on earth irrespective of the consequences." One could make the argument that within nearly three decades of imprisonment, Mandela experienced more freedom living a life of purpose inside a cage than the average person living a life outside one does. Until we implement a system that induces the individual fulfillment of its workers, we will be confined to captivity.

Chapter Ten: On Ideas

"<u>Interviewer</u>: Is it true you are trying to get young black people to be violent to police?

Tupac: No

<u>Interviewer</u>: Were you trying to provoke anybody to do anything in particular, were you trying to provoke or get anyone to do things?

Tupac: Yes

<u>Interviewer</u>: Tell us what?

Tupac: Think …"

- Transcript of Tupac's testimony defending an accusation that his music influenced the murder of a policeman.

The Hitler Regime in Nazi Germany, The Lenin Regime in the Union of Soviet Socialist Republic, and Apartheid Era in South Africa shared a number of oppressive tactics. Censorship was a critical component of each campaign. An idea is the single most powerful force in the world. It is infectious. Once we are exposed to it, it is impossible to completely disregard. Whether true or false, a piece of us wants to verify it. For these political structures, eliminating the spread of rebellious ideas was imperative. Regardless if it is of political, entrepreneurial, or social nature the power of an idea should be well-regarded.

Historically, censorship has been used as a tool by governments to regulate the moral and political lives of their population. It was viewed as a duty of the government to shape the character of the people. To achieve this, they understood how important it was to monitor the spread of ideas. It is usually not the sword that sparks a revolution but the voices of a few men. In modern time, legislation such as the first amendment [from the United States Constitution] has been set in place. Laws structured around this liberty restricts the government's ability to regulate free expression and aid in raising the overall consciousness of the population. Yet it has not stopped governments from being instrumental in quarantining ideas. Alternative tactics allow governments to be equally effective at this task.

The most efficient way to control a group of people is to keep them unaware and distracted. Two methods are commonly used to achieve this. I) The first is misdirection. Keep the population so focused on meaningless events they are oblivious to substantial ones. Essentially fill the population with so many ideas they cannot focus on the pivotal ones. II) Project hope. If a government can give the people just enough hope to keep them content they can create the notion they are entertaining unwanted ideas. Public assistance programs keep the population from questioning the underlining causes of generational poverty. During times of injustice public speakers are televised promoting the issue is important. They make promises of repercussion and reformation. In these cases, it seems like the issues are being attended to but there are no long-term results and the idea eventually fades. Governments exude a great amount of effort to relinquish the public of the power that lies within our ideas.

Ideas are equally impactful in business. Every business started as an idea in someone's mind. For many of us this is where our ideas stay. No matter how unpolished or raw our ideas are, we should take the initial steps to manifest them. The power of an idea in politics is its ability to go viral, it's power in business is its ability to defy reality. Ideas help us redefine our limitations. They expand human boundaries. Someone living during the pre-aviation era would find it hard to conceptualize the idea that humans can fly. Today we barely think twice about it. Commonly, it is the ideas that scare us, that others deem as impossible that contribute the most to advancing the human experience.

From a social aspect, ideas effect our perception of ourselves and others. It corresponds to the law of attraction. If someone consistently declares who they are and what they will become, it will eventually take shape. Our actions are influenced by our thoughts. Therefore, what we believe we can achieve is of greater importance than the strategy or skill set we possess to achieve it. Our idea of our self is what we ultimately become. Additionally, it influences the perception of others. i.e.) – If an athlete of great talent and skill relative to his era consistently declares he is the greatest ever, it is only a matter of time before someone supports this claim. One person turns to two and so on. The truth is distinctions such as "I am the best" are subjective. It is not so much a matter of statistics but a matter of perception. The concept of best will always be debatable. The key is to become good or relevant enough to place yourself in the conversation. Yet it all stems from us wholeheartedly believing our idea of who we are.

Among all its abilities, an idea's greatest strength is it never dies. The idea of a person lives on long after they are dead. It has the potential to inspire those who encounter it greater than it did the creator. Subsequently a man's ideas will always be more powerful than the actual man. No one quite knows what happens to an idea deferred and we should never hope to find out.

Chapter Eleven: On Gender Roles

"Differences are not intended to separate, to alienate. We are different precisely in order to realize our need of one another."
- Desmond Tutu

A dragonfly has six legs, yet it cannot walk. Our anatomy does not dictate our role in the universe. Although the physical makeup of men and women are similar, it is our individual niches that have resulted in humanities preeminence. Society has proposed men and women have separate roles. These roles are characterized by masculine and feminine traits. Yet, they work equally to advance the human agenda. The gender roles of women and men are naturally derived. They are not a social construct. It is the perceived supremacy appointed to gender roles that has been socially composed. When two similar structures exist, it is human nature to declare one more dominant. It is better to view these roles as different, and not in competition.

Gender roles are built neither on our anatomy nor social prevalence. They are built on our natural inclinations. Women instinctually yearn to nurture and cultivate. Men desire to provide and protect. This remains true even if these inclinations are being directed towards the same sex. As a result, men and women will continue to embrace these roles in society not as a requirement, but because they provide a sense of fulfillment. This must be considered when we contemplate redefining gender roles. Feminism is the pursuit of equal rights, free expression, economic and social acknowledgement of women. It should not be viewed as a fight to prove women's dominance. This distinction is critical in determining the outcome of the movement. The former will result in the assimilation of the gender role of women. An attempt to prove women's dominance will result in women mirroring the role of men. Women will essentially attempt to be better and more successful at the gender role of men, than men are. Consequently, we will lose an entire aspect of the human dynamic as the traits and tasks aligned with women will begin to disappear. There is no reason for this conformity. The gender role of women is no less significant than the gender role of men. When we internalize this, we can understand why a woman can aspire to marry, have children, cook, uplift and support her significant other and be no less of a feminist.

Matriarch societies like those of Hyenas and Lions help put this in context. In female dominated social groups like these, traditional gender roles are reversed. Women hunt while men stay with the cubs. Even in a matriarchy, could an argument not be made that it is unfair for women to work while men stay home?

Regardless of the tasks and which gender they belong to, if we attach an uneven level of appreciation to them an argument will be formed that one side is being exploited.

It is important to acknowledge that attributes aligned with gender roles are not exclusive. Restricting access to these attributes only lengthens the gap in how we perceive gender roles. The most impactful restrictions are placed on sexuality and emotional transparency. Women are unable to be sexual beings, like men are unable to be emotional beings. Stigmatizing these attributes, prohibits us from being able to express ourselves. We develop alternative ways to cope with this inability. However, this longing still exists. Thus, we subconsciously envy the opposite gender role because they have a capacity that we do not. Envy incites competition. Our gender roles will not be viewed as equal until we accept the idea that using attributes from the opposite gender role as outlets of expression does not compromise our ability to identify with our own.

To be classified as different requires uniqueness. It means you are in possession of something the perceiver is lacking. Differences in our gender roles are our strength. Our attributes complement each other. What one gender role lacks the opposite compensates. Our diversity perpetuates tenacity and ingenuity. The human dynamic is bilateral. We must glorify both components. They are two sides of the same coin. Its overall value is inseparable.

Chapter Twelve: On Authority

"Quis custodiet ipsos custodes?"
- Juvenal

In 2014, The United States had less than five percent (4.4%) of the world's population, yet almost twenty-five percent (22%) of the world's total prison population. The argument of good or bad cop is a trivial debate. The focal point of our dilemma is the presence of an overall defective system. We incentivize the social position of a police officer like corporations incentivize their salesman. Placing quotas and commission on tickets and arrests, provides alternate motives to target individuals.

When prison in a country becomes such a lucrative business it must follow the same economic principles as any other business. Demand for prisoners are a factor of profitability. As a police officer, what now becomes your primary goal? To protect and serve the community or to profit from it. You now must distinguish a line of morality that is already embedded in the title of your position. Perhaps it is not always a conflict of interest, but in such an altruistic position a police officer should never have to make a choice based on how it will personally affect them. Yet, job expectations force them to make this decision every day.

There are many pieces to this puzzle, not just police officers and it is worth noting they each should be held equally accountable for the result. "Quis custodiet ipsos custodes?" is a Latin phrase coined by Roman poet Juvenal. It translates in English as "Who will guard the guards themselves?" or "Who watches the watchmen?" The phrase embodies the philosophical analysis of power. The question illustrates why the concept of authority is inherently flawed. Authority is structured on the idea individuals can fairly monitor and enforce law and order among other individuals. The concept ignores the fact that the enforcement agents are only human themselves. Therefore, they have similar bias, tempers, egos, problems and societal expectations as the people they are regulating. The effectiveness of a system based on flawed people regulating other flawed people is questionable. Enlightenment thinkers Thomas Hobbes and Montesquieu were instrumental figures in political philosophy. In his writing, *Leviathan*, Hobbes proposes that humans are innately cruel, selfish, and greedy. He argues that social positions such as police officers are required to keep humanity from being in a constant state of war and chaos. Instinctually human motivation is guided by self-interest. Hobbes reasoning for the need of authoritative figures is the same reason we must reform the current system.

Human nature does not change when we provide individuals with a title, list of laws, and weapons. For this reason, occupants of these positions need stringent and continuous training, evaluation, and regulation. Montesquieu acknowledges the possibility for corruption in authoritative and governing systems with his idea "separation of power." This idea withdraws supreme authority from any single sector and spreads it across different branches. Montesquieu's theoretical invention is perhaps the most fulfilling answer to our conundrum. Three watchmen, with three different sectors of power, completely separate and without interdependent incentive can watch each other. Fully expending this ideology to all government allocated authoritative systems and their positions is the first step to an effective system. By doing this we decrease the misuse of power and enforce accountability for actions.

We can use Hobbes's and Montesquieu's mentioned intellectual contributions as a reference for the psychology of authority. These combined ideas lead to a significant conclusion – Even within a system, single individuals are incapable of reasonably and responsibly maintaining and exerting authority; Supervisory systems are needed to supplement this inability.

In 1973, Dr. Zimbardo conducted the Stanford Experiment which heavily supports this claim. The experiment randomly split a group of screened men into prisoners and guards. The results showed that the titles distributed to the men influenced their behavior. Guards responded to their perceived authority by being overly aggressive. Prisoners responded to their lack of authority by being submissive. As individuals set into their social positions it becomes a part of their identity. By allowing a group of people to enforce the law they will essentially themselves feel lawless.

Our current policing system does not work. This is partially because we are trying to corporationalize a naturally benevolent position. In doing so we are placing people in a position they have no true affinity or passion for. It is also partially because humans were not made to govern each other. Our natural inclinations contradict the needed traits to fairly regulate. Still, the need for this position exists and we must take the necessary steps to address these underlining issues.

Chapter Thirteen: On Nostalgia

"The present is the only thing a man can give up.
because it is the only thing which he has, and that a man
cannot lose a thing he does not have."
- **Marcus Aurelius**

Einstein's law of relativity proposes our perception of time is relative; the observer is the most important factor in using the concept to accurately rationalize the world around us. Adjusting our outlook on time enables us to reach a state of tranquility. It is the gateway for growth. If neither can be constructed in the present - it is detrimental to romanticize of things you formerly possessed and equally unbeneficial to fanaticize of future successes. Memories from our past are better off locked in a vault. They are often only a shell of reality; a mural of the parts of people and experiences we yearn to cling to. Their lessons have been extracted and are already subconsciously apart of us. Subsequently, holding onto these memories are only time consuming and a cowardly attempt to gain happiness.

Fantasizing of the future is similarly a lost effort. Events that have not yet come to fruition should be worked on today and every day until they are manifested. Our present has the ability to dwarf our past, and allows us to create a greater future. Therefore, all of our energy should be placed on actions we can take in the present.

The memories we are most fond of keeping are those of old friendships. Any relation left unattended, no matter how long the duration will result in a loss of intimacy. Hazlitt expresses this idea in his essay *On the Pleasure of Hating*. He states "Old friendships are like meats served up repeatedly, cold, comfortless, and distasteful. The stomach turns against them. Either constant intercourse and familiarity breed weariness and contempt; if we meet again after an interval of absence, we appear no longer the same." We must ask ourselves why we routinely mold our memories into what we want them to be. Subconsciously, we are making an instinctual effort to resist change. It is our only combative weapon against the wrath of time. In our memories, we're able to return to times in our life before we underwent the undesirable experiences that shaped us into the person we are today.

Change brings one guarantee, and that is for the change to be perceived as positive, negative, or uninvited in someone's opinion. As we apply this concept to how time effects our relationships, we arrive at the conclusion that we should go against our natural instinct and leave unattained friendships untouched because the person we venture in search of will no longer exist. Our memories are just that. Screenshots of times in our lives that no longer exist.

When we cannot accept the past, it is natural for us to place our hopes and dreams into the future. But hope can be a dangerous pursuit. Roman Emperor Marcus Aurelius, debatably the most powerful man to live, was a student of Stoic Philosophy and makes the motif of time a recurring theme in his reflections. In his writing, *Meditations*, he states, "remember the rapidity with which things pass by and disappear, both the things which are and the things which are produced. For existence is like a flowing river, and the activities of things are in constant change, and the causes work in infinite varieties; And consider this boundless abyss of the past and of the future in which all things disappear. How then is he not a fool who is puffed up with such things or plagued about them and makes himself miserable? for they vex him only for a time, and a short time." Aurelius is making a reference to the idea the past and future are abstract. Both are unobtainable today and therefore have the capacity to never be available. Placing our emotions and faith in either facilitates disappointment. The actions we take today are what shapes our future and past. If these actions are advantageous, we are relieved the past did not become the present and we are satisfied with what has become the future.

Time encompasses a great paradigm. It is the bringer of truth and the holder of lies. It offers two options. You either die a hero or live long enough to see yourself become the villain. The past contains our memories. It allows us to freely repaint canvasses the way we envision them. The future holds our dreams; with them the capacity for failure and criticism. Somewhere between both is reality. This reality is the present, and it is the only option we have full control over. The people, events, and materials we are in possession of today are the only things we may claim ownership of. Things that have been lost and cannot be replaced should be deemed as the equivalent of us never owning them. Things that are not being worked on daily should be deemed as never coming to fruition. All energy not being placed on the present is energy being wasted.

Chapter Fourteen: On Anxiety & Perfection

"It's not that perfection cannot be achieved. It's that it's so hard to stop there."
- Robert Brault

It is challenging to comprehend why humanity struggles so greatly with anxiety. We spend hours, days, and nights worrying about situations that may never occur or will be experienced in a fraction of the time in which we contemplate them. Anxiety is the emotion we seemingly should have the most control over, yet it is the one that eludes our understanding. To analyze how anxiety effects humans, we must examine how it effects our animal counterparts. Undomesticated animals experience anxiety differently than humans. Their experience is directly connected to their survival. Unlike humans, most wild animals only experience the feelings of nervousness, fear, and stress when they are placed in life or death situations. When else would they? Animals live substantially simpler lives than humans. Their goals are survival and reproduction. As a result, they have no need to use such a drastic emotion as often as humans do.

Anxiety is a mental reaction. It is how our mind tells our body we are going to lose something of importance if we do not act. The problem is we view too many things as important. Conclusively, we have created an extensive level of anxiety in our everyday lives. The way humans experience anxiety is the equivalent to an oblivious middle school student ringing the fire alarm when there is no fire; our anxious reactions come from man-made events. Interviews, tests, public speaking, project deadlines and similar events perpetuate the social expectations we have placed on ourselves.

Anxiety is only an emotion and therefore it solely exists in our mind. It is controllable and can be manifested however we choose. To do this we must accept the following I) For humans, anxiety is most often a consequence of our persistent pursuit of perfection. II) The most debilitating component of anxiety is its ability to induce a pseudo-overwhelming feeling. By discrediting this feeling we can conquer this emotion. III) Humans experience real anxious reactions and false anxious reactions. We must use "physical relativeness" to distinguish the two.

To be human is to be flawed. It is in our nature to make mistakes. We stumble, we miscalculate, and we make less than efficient choices. Yet we are integrated in a society that teaches us that perfection is obtainable. It shames those who fail and commends those who perform well. This creates the pressure to never underperform and more detrimentally to feel defective when we do. We must accept that it is ok to make mistakes. We are not machines and our lives are filled with self-made errors. If we fail, we will live. Tomorrow we will still possess the capacity to create the same or a better opportunity. As a result, we can rid ourselves of the idea we lose something of importance if we fail, and view these events as challenges to gain something of importance. Succeed or fail, if you continue to exhibit similar character and habits similar opportunities will constantly present themselves.

Anxiety evokes several feelings. The most impactful is the feeling of being overwhelmed. This feeling comes from how we view the anxiety inducing situation. We view these situations as having no limit or end. Interviews are notorious anxiety inducing events. Answering questions can be practiced. Public speaking can be rehearsed. However, we cannot prepare for the type or number of questions we will be asked. As a result, we will never obtain the sentiment of feeling prepared. This creates an unhealthy cycle; the more we practice the more anxious we become. This limitless feeling is false and must be discarded. Interviews, tests and similar events are composed of a set amount of questions. These questions can only be asked in different ways. An interviewer may ask – what are your skills? How would you deal with an irate customer? How do you work on a team? – are these not the same question? Although these events may seem endless, they are timed. Our lives are finite and consequently everything comes to an end. Because of this factor the burden is held by the judger and not the one being judged. If we focus on the essential content and the limited ways it can be manipulated we can mitigate the feeling of being overwhelmed and put our anxiety to rest.

We use our senses to paint a picture of reality. But what happens when our senses betray us? If we were offered a piece of fruit with our eyes blindfolded and hands bonded, we would be forced to construct the reality of this fruit on its scent. Yet the object can be masked in perfume. The expectations that create anxiety have been implanted in our mind. By the time we reach our adolescence our mind is incapable of differentiating real anxious reactions from false anxious reactions. To distinguish which reactions are an illusion, we must use physical relativeness. Once again let's examine an interview. When you are in the lobby waiting for your interviewers, ask yourself who else here is experiencing similar feelings to those that I am experiencing. Is the receptionist nervous? Ask yourself this again in the interview room. What feelings are the individual across the table experiencing? Are they fearful? You will quickly reach the conclusion the people around you are not. A similar question can be asked when you are traveling to your exam. Are the people on this bus having similar feelings of anxiety? If not, then how can these feelings be defined as real? We must realize that while we are experiencing paralyzing anxiety little to no one around us is. These are false anxious reactions built on social expectations. Now consider a natural disaster such as an earthquake. Imagine how the people around you react. Their anxiety and feelings of fear will mirror your own. These events and similar events induce real anxious reactions. Epictetus, a slave turned Stoic Philosophy teacher references this idea in his writing *The Enchiridion*. He wrote: "It's not the accident that distresses this person because it doesn't distress another person; it is the judgment which he makes about it." Epictetus is explaining that if the sentiment of distress a person feels is not felt by the people around that person, the feeling does not exist. This feeling stems from their personal attachment and perception of the event.

Humans face a great deal of anxiety daily. It is naive to believe society will lessen its expectations to compensate for this. As a result, we must change how we view anxiety or succumb to a life outlined with regret, doubt, and recurring failure.

The observer is never as broken as the artist; this is what gives art life. Most times, it takes someone more broken than ourselves to make us realize just how much fixing we need.

Chapter Fifteen: On Kindness

"Be soft. Do not let the world make you hard. Do not let pain make you hate. Do not let the bitterness steal your sweetness. Take pride that even though the rest of the world may disagree, you still believe it to be a beautiful place."
- Kurt Vonnegut, Jr.

Fear is no stronger than love. All emotions are malleable. They are only as strong as their possessor. We choose to take the lower road. In the presence of adversity and criticism we react by abandoning our inclination to love. It is easier to respond to evil with evil, in the process we ignorantly fill the world with more of what we are trying to rid it of. We argue that it is a necessary response. Kindness is equivalent to weakness. But this reasoning is of a selfish nature. We are in control of our own actions. We cannot choose how people treat us but we can choose how we respond. Their actions define them; our response defines us. We have made it acceptable to react to hate with feelings of equal sentiment. Until we gather the courage to meet pain with kindness, our society will be blanketed with a culture of animosity and hatefulness.

We view life as a race to the top. Consequently, our strength lies in our ability to challenge and undermine each other. German philosopher Friedrich Nietzsche would support this idea. In his writing *The Genealogy of Morality* he proposes there are two branches of morality - master and slave morality. Nietzsche praises the master morality, stating it is the morality for the strong willed. The morality justifies the idea of using oppression and fear to gain power and respect. He brags the users of this morality "rightly evokes fear in those who are not their equal and a respectful distance in those who are." Nietzsche explains the morality is built to perpetuate power, ability, wealth, and pride.

Today, the pursuit of similar values are instilled within us. The morality aligns with the culture of hate we have created to facilitate our personal gain. If we further examine the master morality it becomes evident that this morality is rooted in vanity and hubris. Nietzsche proclaims the morality gains its goodness from the "celebration of one's [the user's] own greatness and power." The morality focuses on inequality and self-advancement by any means. Contrarily, Nietzsche defines the slave morality as weak and feeble. It is derived from the user's discontentment with the master's morality. It values altruism, humility, patience and in one word – universal utility. It solely exists as the user's way to cope with its inability to change its positioning in society. If we look at Nietzsche's moralities holistically we can pinpoint his own value system.

Marcus Aurelius, the renowned Roman Emperor and student of stoicism would be skeptical of this philosophy. In his writing, *Meditations,* he states "Alexander the Great and his mule driver both died and the same thing happened to both. They were absorbed alike into the life force of the world, or dissolved alike into atoms." This uncovers a critical flaw in Nietzsche's morality assessment. He proclaims the master morality retains its supremacy because it promotes strength, power, and control. When in fact, this exhibits its inferiority. Everything gained from these attributes will die with their processor or curse them with a dishonorable legacy.

Alexander the Great will forever be linked to murder, rape, and greed. Holidays created to commemorate conquerors such as Christopher Columbus will forever be questioned. Victories connected to Adolf Hitler will forever be symbolic of hate. Likewise, dishonorable legacies will plague all powerful man who gained their position from stepping on others. The slave morality promotes magnanimity and kindness. These attributes aid in making the world better as a whole. These attributes do not wither. After its possessor dies they live through the people they helped. People will aspire to spread these attributes because of how much they were impacted by them.   The road to self-advancement does not run in the opposite direction of altruism. We can build ourselves up without tearing others down. But we can only unravel the density of hate we've created with patience and kindness.

Tupac once said "If you're not dark inside and you come to this world, it'll turn you dark... and if you really have sunshine inside you, it's not good to play in the dark. It's just gonna extinguish your fire." The people in the world are not dark nor is the world itself, evilness spawns from the misunderstanding of these two entities. Our lives are filled with situations we perceive as unfortunate. It is these events that taint humanity, but only because we choose to react with negative sentiments. We take this negative energy and spread them amongst people. This results in more negative responses and unfortunate events creating a cycle. If your co-worker has expressed ill will towards you and you react with an equally ill response what have you done but created a hostile environment and tended to your own ego. Both you and the coworker will now spread negativity to other co-workers and people in your lives. But if you react with kindness it will baffle your co-worker. They may not respond with kindness initially but it will sit on their conscious with a force heavier than a boulder resting upon a mountain. They will wonder what secrets you possess to respond with kindness. They will question their actions and eventually change them as they realize their ill actions have no effect on you. They will aspire to gain the peace you have. A peace they can only achieve through compassion and endurance. This will reflect in the way they interact with people in all aspects of their lives.

Being emotionless does not make you tougher. Just as being full of emotions does not make you weak. Emotions are needed to help us express ourselves. Although it is tempting and seemingly satisfying to spread negative emotions among those who we interact with we must reframe from this action. The world is in dire need of love and kindness. This is a result of us letting hate control us. If we do not acknowledge the impact it has historically had on us and where it will lead us we will pay a great price for our selfishness.

Chapter Sixteen: On Technology and Social Media

"I see humans but no humanity."
- Jason Donohue

It is an undeniable truth; technology has contributed greatly to the advancement of humanity. It has made our society a faster and more efficient place. It's had an unprecedented impact on healthcare, banking, communication, education, traveling, and virtually any aspect of life we can name. In a sentence - it has changed the world. But like any powerful tool, it possesses the potential to bring both positive and negative change. Its presence presents a challenge to humanity. It has altered the human dynamic by placing new standards on humanity. It demands we become quicker, more thorough, more like metal. It has unlocked doors of information that are accessible with the click of a button. Simultaneously it has barricaded them with fences of mind numbing programs and advertisements crafted to promote consumerism. It has produced ways to explore the universe and with the same designs created weapons to destroy it. It serves as an example the sword is only as liberating or as enslaving as its wielder.

It has had a subtle, yet dangerous impact on how we interact with each other. It has made the world smaller while creating more distance between us. Social media has become a critical pillar of our society. It is such a routine part of our everyday lives we are blind to how much of ourselves we invest in it. First, we must acknowledge the positive components of social media. It creates a virtual place to stay connected to friends and family. It gives us a platform to share and express ourselves. It has revolutionized how we promote our talents and businesses. It serves as an alternative means to spread information that is censored from mainstream media outlets. These factors make social media praise worthy. However, they are like diamonds on a mining site. They do not compare to the destructive impact social media has and will continue to bear on our society.

The dangers of social media can be attributed to the following I) Our virtual selves have become an extended version of our physical selves. We connect our identity and sense of self to these social applications. II) We are sharing too much of ourselves. The more we live through these applications the less we're able to enjoy life and live in the moment. III) Social media is so accessible we are unaware of how dependent we are on it and how unproductive we have become because of it.

The impact social media has on our perception of ourselves is detrimental to our happiness. No matter how much we attempt to dispute it, we connect how we feel about ourselves to our followers, likes, and comments. They are indicators of how much the world accepts us. This is particularly dangerous because it is an endless pursuit. If you post a picture that gets a high level of likes, you will be satisfied for a while, but if your next post does not achieve the same level or higher, you will begin to wonder what happened. Like an addiction, you will chase the feeling you received after getting your record topping likes. You embark on a roller coaster ride composed of highs and lows. Your eagerness to reach that level again heightens and the means you are willing to take to achieve it widens.

We process the followers, the likes, the views like we do numbers in any virtual program. They are metrics of how well we are doing. We associate higher numbers with winning. But this idea does not merge well with reality. Life is complicated and its value is immeasurable.

Social media takes our need for validation to new depths. Using it as a means to be seen makes us feel more invisible. It allows us to construct the life we want online, deterring us from creating it in the real world. We build a parallel reality in which everyone is posting only the positive components of their lives. Excluding the hardships and adversity taken to reach these evokes a general longing for instant success.

Unconsciously our sense of happiness is relative. The more we see other people's lives – accomplishments, relationships, materials, jobs the more we measure our progress on them. The more we expose ourselves to other people's lives the more we will feel like we are lacking something. In a similar way, it creates a longing to have the things we see others have. Human desire is, by large, unmeditated desire. Rene Girad referred to this as Mimetic Desire. It is the idea that all our desires are unknowingly borrowed from others. Social media influences everything from the physical attributes we find attractive, the clothes we like, even the decision to be in a relationship. Social media contributes in shaping our desires based on popular opinion. Ultimately, it colludes any innate desires we have, making our choices heavily constructed on what society deems popular.

Social media hinders our ability to build and maintain our real-world relationships. The more people who have virtual access to our lives the less emphasis we place on the people who are tangibly in it. We begin to view people in general as more disposable and replaceable. We are less willing to pursue and fight for the true bonds in our real lives. We replace the longing for people we have real world connections with the synthetic feelings we can achieve through social media. The imitated feelings we receive from social media does not satisfy this longing but it masks it just enough for us to forget or replace the authentic feeling we are craving.

This is a key component why our generation has become so prone to ignoring each other, there is an abundance of synthetic attention and care that can now be obtained without even having to step outside. The problem is this synthetic substitute derives from shallow desires and values, therefore it is of the lowest quality. Most if not all the effects of social media are subconscious. We do not actively register the comments, messages, and compliments as adequate substitutes for the presence of the people who truly know and care about us, but it greatly assists in preventing us from realizing how important they are.

Social media creates indirect transparency. Prior to social media we were able to choose the things we allowed in our reality. With social media, the world has become smaller. If someone is ignoring us, an ex-partner is in a new relationship, or an undesirable event occurs social media forces these things into our reality. Our inability to block out things of this nature from our reality is detrimental to our mental health. A "keep out" component in our lives is essential. It allows us to effectively create and manage a sphere of happiness.

Indirect transparency deters us from a closure process. We are living in a world with hurt people that have placed band aids over deep lacerations. No one is truly healing. An athlete who gets injured cannot heal by going directly back to the practice field. Rest or shutting down is just as important to the rehabilitation process as exercise. We must shut out these undesirable ideas in order to create a healthier reality.

Social media dilutes our experiences by compelling us to live our lives for and through others. Instead of attending parties, festivals and events to enjoy ourselves and the company of our friends we go semi-motivated by our chance to document our experience for others. We are not enjoying the moment because we are concerned about showing people how much we are enjoying it. In the process, we get a less than optimal experience. Subsequently this grants the watchers the ability to live vicariously through the people at the event. A person can now be content with staying home and watching what's going on as their entertainment instead of partaking in activities themselves. Ultimately no one is fully in the moment. This dilution spreads to other areas of our lives. Allowing the world to have so much access to our lives diminishes our mystic.

Stoic philosopher Seneca alludes to this idea in his writing *Letters from a Stoic*. He states, "To be everywhere is to be nowhere." The more people we divulge our lives to the less meaning it begins to hold, the less special it feels to those tangibly in it. i.e.) If you give advice to a friend, a large portion of its impact derives from it being personal. This person believes this advice was customized for their situation. This one of one feeling is the consoling component of the advice. If this same person goes on your social media profile and sees the same advice you just gave them, it will undermine its previous effect. Social media makes us somewhat relevant to everyone, and simultaneously meaningful to no one.

Social media has fostered a culture that focuses neither on quality or quantity, but quickness. Our longing for instant gratification is resulting in oversaturation and water downed results. We are taking shortcuts to receive instant acknowledgement. However, the quicker we obtain it the quicker it fades. We no longer cherish anything because we are already anticipating what's next.

Social media places an emphasis on self. The pictures, stories, and quotes we post all focus on our importance in the world. If we pick a profile at random the majority of the individual's posts will be connected to at least one of the following I) Money & materialism – in the form of clothes, jewelry, cars, houses and other coveted objects. II) Attractiveness – in the form of self-portraits and self-videos that focus on highlighting physical features III) Skills & accolades – in the form of awards, degrees, and tutorials IV) Events & location – in the form of pictures and videos in social settings, pictures of food and location tagging. V) Relationships – in the form of pictures and videos of friends, family and significant others. Our entire online experience can be summed up by one statement – World look at me and what I have accomplished. Look at what I have that is better than yours. Look at what I can do that you can't do and look at what I have that you don't have. This mitigates our sentiment that the world and life is bigger than ourselves. Consequently, our perspectives focus less on how we can help others and change the world and more on how we can prove to the world we are here.

Lastly, social media is time consuming. It overlaps with our real lives which makes it difficult for us to indicate it as a distraction. Contrarily, this is why it is so effective. It combines the components of reality television, celebrity gossip, comedy, consumerism, and other unproductive entertainment. All which are fine in moderation but social media packs them together to be explored endlessly at our discretion. Therefore, at any point in time we have the option to place our energy in roaming this fantasy world in place of investing it in productive tasks. There is no longer time for reflection. The reflection portion of our lives is what helps us see our mistakes. It allows us to value the people in them. It allows us to value our journey and decide our next steps. If time for reflection is not available, growth is unobtainable.

If it is not already, social media will be the greatest happiness deterrent in our society. Critics will counter this argument with an overtly simple response - its only social media. Consider how much time we spend on social media - building relationships and broadcasting our lives. We interact with more people on social media per day than we do in our everyday lives.

People have more access to us via social media than they do in reality. As a result, it is arguably more "real", more full of social interaction, ideas, and perceptions than our real lives. These applications have a massive impact on the psychology of ourselves, others and the world. If not consciously monitored they will destroy any hope we have at a fulfilled life.

Chapter Seventeen: On Spirituality

"Just as a candle cannot burn without fire, men cannot live without a spiritual life"
- **Buddha**

Scientist propose at the universe's inception, it was infinitely small, infinitely hot, and infinitely dense. The universe began expanding and cooling tremendously. For billions of years our universe populated stars, galaxies, and most importantly our Solar System which encompasses planet Earth, the only planet with the required astronomical balance to harbor life. This is referred to as the Big Bang Theory. Scientist also propose that the inhabitants of our planet acquire physical modifications that allow them to adapt to their environment. This is called the Theory of Evolution. These theories are the most popular scientific theories used to explain the origin of the human experience. Additionally, they are often used as arguments to disclaim components of spirituality. However, if we focus on the level of coincidence required to make these theories possible, it is evident they are proponents of it.

The development of a planet with the ability to maintain humanity, encompassed in a universe that cannot sustain life is in the truest sense of the word - a miracle. The same can be said about the transition of primitive animals to cognitive humans who learned to design and construct pyramids, bridges, towers and wireless internet connectivity. Scientist believe two entities make up the majority of the universe - dark matter accounts for approximately 25% of the universe and dark energy accounts for about 70%. Together they compose almost 95% of the universe. The only problem is scientist do not know what dark matter or dark energy is. Situations like this allow us to see science is a tool used to gain an understanding of the world, but it does not have the ability to fully explain it. For those answers, we must place our understanding in a higher source.

Philosophy like science is often viewed as anti-spiritual. Both science and philosophy use theories to attempt to define the world around us. Both develop hypothesis, apply them and observe the results. Both fail miserably at their task. The development of both came from our fascination with the complicated world we live in. They should be viewed as methods used to help us feel safe, confident, and enjoy life. Ultimately, they are ways to cope with our inability to satisfy one of our greatest inclinations – to control things we don't understand.

Our perception of spirituality is heavily based on what we view in the world as good or bad. Among the most popular questions is - how can there be a higher being if he endorses so much tragedy and destruction. Is pain not love? From the perspective of the less wise the answer is no. But consider this scenario. When a child misbehaves, and displays habitual actions in which a superior knows will have a detrimental effect on its growth and future, is it not the superior's duty to intervene? The superior does what it deems fit in that moment to alter the path of the less wise, sometimes at the cost of their own happiness. The less wise cannot fathom how the actions taken by the superior are in their best interest because they have no understanding of the knowledge the superior holds. It will see the superior as unworthy of their title until it gains a better understanding of its actions. This is a simple concept to grasp when viewing from a parent/child perspective but to grasp it on a spiritual level we must go deeper. The child has the capacity to one day understand the doings of its superior which leads to reconciliation and appreciation. As humans, we do not and will never have the capacity to understand the complex actions of a higher being.

Compare an ant's society to that of humanities. Think about how complex an ant believes his world to be. They have families and everyday duties, systems, a social hierarchy, rules and an overall way of life. They wake up every day believing the world they have created is governed by some logic and reasoning. Yet they will never be able to fathom the world humans have created. Our metric and irrigation system, math, technology, aerospace innovation, and numerous other inventions dwarf their entire being. They were not created to understand this, but created to live and continue the life they were given. It is not in their capacity to understand it but more importantly it is not in their capacity to question it. As humans, we have been granted this ability to question. We have used it to advance humanity through innovation but it is debatable if we are truly worthy or ready for it.

Plato examines the relationship between morality and spirituality in his writing *Euthyphro* by introducing the Euthyphro dilemma. The dilemma is derived from this question – "are good things good because God commands them as good, or does God command them as good because they are good." If the first portion of the statement is true, God is the standard for what is good and bad, even if he commands horrific actions these actions should be seen as good. If the second portion is true, this means God defines what is good based on an outside standard. Since we agree our world is composed of good and bad there must be an outside force that allows for bad to exist. Plato is proposing that both of these scenarios cannot be true because they are contradictory. The writing ends inconclusively. Jay-z rephrases this question in his song *No Church for the Wild*. He asks "Is Pious pious 'cause God loves pious?" It is a question Plato proposes but never answers. Not by choice, but because he is aware he is incapable of providing an answer. He understands the answer is of divine nature and beyond human comprehension. The

Euthyphro dilemma is a prime example of how we should use philosophy in relation to theism. Philosophy is used to break ideas down as much as humanly possible to achieve universal ways to view and deal with them. When we examine ideas our minds are not built to understand it is a useless tool.

The idea of life is the greatest paradox we will encounter. How can something so plentiful and of abundance be so individually valuable. On a planet with over 7 billion people, each life holds immense value and importance to its owner. It is impossible to even begin to comprehend the job of a God. Each action he takes in the life of one person influences the lives of others - both of immediate and distant relationship. By giving something to one person he must take it from someone else. If you simply attempt to imagine the string of actions and effects caused by moving one piece you can find some contentment in the impracticality of only cheerful outcomes. Gaining a higher sense of spirituality comes from understanding life is set at an equilibrium.

We cannot develop an appreciation for any sentiment without the presence of the opposite feeling. To be happy we must feel pain, for every day there must be night, to enjoy life there must be death. Our joy is derived from this limited feeling. Spirituality is accepting life is constantly at balance and having faith that the dark times are governed by reasoning and one day will be replaced with light.

Chapter Eighteen: On Money & Value

"Some people are so poor; all they have is money."
- **Patrick Meager**

The most coveted object in a society will also be the most destructive. The pursuit of monetary success has historically been characterized by division and greed. The desire for wealth has resulted in betrayal and murder. It has destroyed relationships with family and friends. It has been the motive for freedom jeopardizing actions. In short - the cynical and sinister sentiment it incites corrupts humanity. Its power lies in its ability to make us forget the things that are truly important to us. The idea of money is stronger than the practical use of it.

This creates two fundamental problems I) we integrate invaluable factors of our lives with a value system that was constructed for material things. Subconsciously we put a price on the people in our lives. We should have two separate value systems. One that measures people and their importance and one that measures money and its ability to purchase commodities and goods. The former should always undermine the latter. II) The idea of money is held in high regard by both those who possess it and those who do not. We must mitigate the idea of money so it can be valued and used in a practical way.

Money can turn the most important person in your life into your enemy. We cannot control a person's feelings toward us. We must consciously divide the value we place on money from the value we place on the people in our lives. They are not in the same tier. There is no circumstance in which the people in our lives are less important than money. This is easy to forget as ego, greed, and our desire for status and materialism arise. We must remember these people are often the motivation for our monetary pursuit. It has been their friendship, encouragement, and guidance that has aided in our financial gain. Therefore, losing one of them is costlier than losing any amount of money.

Outside of the cost of living, money is a tool. It is printed to be used on yourself and others. It is an instrument that allows us to afford experiences and create memories. If you have an abundance of money but lack important people in your life to share it with it takes away from its usefulness and furthermore its value. This is not to say we should use it carelessly but we should be thoughtful and persistent when approaching situations that mix money and people. For example, granting requests for physical money is not an ideal action. The requester will become content and a dependency will develop. The nature of your relationship will change as the person believes they are entitled to this. If not, why did you begin granting their request? Instead decline their request. In place of physical money occasionally buy them gifts. This way you are avoiding the loaner and borrower relationship and still displaying to them that they are more valuable to you than money. The value of money is dependent on the people in our lives and therefore should remain in this lower tier reserved for its capacity to obtain objects.

The idea of money is often detrimental to both those who have limited and unlimited access to it. To effectively utilize and value money we must aspire to reach a balanced point. Operating at either side of the extremes is ineffective. In his writing, *Nicomachean Ethics*, Aristotle refers to this point as the "Golden Mean." He explains that optimality is located between a level of excess and deficiency. At this point we reach the virtuous point that allows us to view and use things wisely. Aristotle provides a list of examples outlining two vices (extremes) and their virtuous point, some of which are below:

Deficiency (Vice)	Mean (Virtue)	Excess (Vice)
Cowardice (lacking confidence)	Courage	Rashness (too much confidence)
Humility (lacking honor)	Proper Pride	Empty Vanity (too much honor)
Boorishness (lacking sense of humor)	Wittiness	Buffoonery (too much sense of humor)

Aristotle explores the pursuit of money and identifies stinginess as the deficient vice and wastefulness as excess vice. He believes the virtuous point is liberality. Both extremes focus on self-interest, perpetuated by the idea of money. When we exert liberality or generosity, we put in context the value of money. We gain a greater sense of our own needs by examining and contributing to the circumstances of others. During this process, we make efficient choices. We manage our money by weighing our own utility against our friends, family, and humanity in general. Aristotle acknowledges to reach the golden mean we often require experience and should not be judged during this journey.

The two vices effect how the groups at each end view and use money. People who have limited access to money fantasize about how it can change their circumstance. They undervalue the life they currently live thinking money will bring a change. The more money they accumulate the more they become frugal and self-interested. The idea of money and the feelings it evokes in the possessor and the people around them become problematic. It initiates a push and pull effect between the person with money and those who remain without it. To an extent any person with new found wealth becomes a money hoarder. They possess a fear of returning to a point where money is scarce. The people around them experience the opposite, they become money spending advocates. They believe this person is entitled to spend more money on the advancement of themselves and others. Eventually the friction created by this disconnect will induce the person with money to realize the true value of it and will allow them to use it practically. However, the time this process takes and losses accrued during it varies.

Similarly, those with unlimited access to money experience a distorted sense of its value. Continual access to money perpetuates an unconscious sense of entitlement. Inhabitants of this extreme vice create a smaller world defined by problems not based on money but expectations and relative social status. Since money is not a factor they live in a very different reality than inhabitants at the other extreme, however they experience adversity and hardships in the same manner. Although the situations they encounter are less dire, the emotions of fear and anxiety they feel are processed the same. Contrary to the other extreme, money is an expectation and is valued in its ability to assist with problems not in its ability to solve them. Although it spawns from different reasons, the idea of money and the self-interest it promotes colludes the practical use of it at both extremes.

To reach the golden mean those at one extreme must experience or be conscious of the troubles of those at the other extreme. The Hegelian Dialectic, derived by the German Philosopher Hegel insists it takes three perspectives to establish an adequate understanding of the subject at hand. Examining the first two perspectives enables us to synthesize the good and bad qualities of both and develop what Hegel refers to as the "Absolute idea." It is only at this point we will be able to develop a system that properly assesses the value and importance of money.

Zig Zilar states "Money will buy you a bed, but not a good night's sleep. A house but not a home. A companion but not a friend." Needless to say – money can buy us many things, but it provides us with nothing.

Chapter Nineteen: On Growth

"We must be willing to let go of the life we planned so as to have the life that is waiting for us."
- Joseph Campbell

The caged bird yearns for freedom. It admires the world it observes outside the cage, but it has grown content with the cage's enticing features. The bird receives food, protection, and love every day. Those who visit the caged bird are intrigued and admire its beauty. The bird has become aware of their expectations and feels responsible for meeting them. It disregards the opportunities and experiences the world has to offer; the bird prefers the cage because of its familiarity. In the process, it has become oblivious to the restricting nature of the cage. It has decided this is its purpose. Resistance to growth can most clearly be understood by looking at the caged bird's dilemma.

We often set a concrete path that we feel obligated to follow. However, it is naive to believe the future version of ourselves will be happy with the aspirations, goals, and mindset of the present version of ourselves. Between the years of present and future, we encounter new experiences, people, and places that will shape who we want to be and what we want to contribute to the world. We will gain a greater sense of self-awareness, a new level of world-awareness, and ultimately mature. As a result, some things that were important to us years ago, will no longer hold the same value. It is better for us to adjust and make changes as needed to incorporate our growth. It is better to view our future as a journey composed of dead ends, hills, valleys, pit stops and U-turns rather than a one-way road forward.

We lack control over the events that take place in our lives, but we control the lessons we extract from them. Embodying this stoic principle aids in advancing our personal development. Logotherapy founder and Existentialism analyst Viktor Frankl stated – "Between stimulus and response there is a space. In that space is our power to choose our response. In our response lies our growth and our freedom." Our freedom to choose how we respond to the events that occur dictates our growth, not our ability to dictate how the events in our lives will occur. Subsequently, using our experiences to adjust our values and goals is a testament to our growth. It is this example of maturity that leads to a fulfilling life.

We should learn from the unfamiliar circumstances we encounter. German Philosopher Hegel was a proponent of the thought we should make learning from uninvited ideas a habit. He believed the insight conducive to our progress is capsulated in uncomfortable and enigmatic places. We should extract lessons from these situations that contribute to our moral disposition and decision making. Our preordained hopes and plans deter us from discovering the ideas that emancipate our full potential.

We can use the life of Mohandas Gandhi as a reference point. Gandhi's early life heavily contrasts the life and impact he would ultimately have. Gandhi was born into a wealthy family, his father was the Prime Minister of Porbander, India. As a child, Gandhi received an exceptional education. When he was 18 years of age, Gandhi traveled to London to study law at University College London. This was a privilege few of his peers could afford. Three years later Gandhi returned to India after passing the bar. Everything in his story up to this point presaged Gandhi to be a prosperous lawyer. If he would have stringently stayed on this path – one in which offered the wealth, and success we desperately crave - history along with his legacy would greatly differ. Instead, upon his arrival back to India, Gandhi experienced a string of events that he embraced and let influence him.

When Gandhi reached Bombay, he was notified his mother had died while he was in London. In the years following his return, Gandhi had a hard time competing against home-bred lawyers who knew more Indian law and charged lower fees. Because of his inability to find consistent work, Gandhi accepted a year-long contract from Dada Abdulla & Co., an Indian firm. The contract required him to travel to South Africa to act on the behalf of a local Indian trader in a commercial dispute. Gandhi's tenure in South Africa is regularly agreed to be the turning point in his life. It was here he faced the racism, prejudice, and discrimination commonly directed toward black South Africans. At one of his court appearances he was asked to remove his turban. He was thrown off a train after refusing to move from the first-class section, although he was holding a valid first class ticket. He was frequently prohibited from checking in many hotels. These unfamiliar and unjust events changed Gandhi's perspective, goals, and values. They contributed to his growth and allowed him to contribute to the progress of society in a deeply personal and unique way.

We must accept we have little influence on the external events that transpire in our lives, yet these events can change the course of our future. Growth is being able to accept the person that you want to be may not be who you are. The person you want to be is a figment of your hopes. The person you are is a manifestation of your experiences. If these two coincide consider yourself fortunate. But if they don't, that is ok.

Our collage of hopes become our cage. We marginalize ourselves by proclaiming who we will be. This is consistent with French philosopher Jean-Paul Sartre idea of living in "Bad Faith." Sartre believes we are prone to forgetting one of our greatest capacities - free will. We become fixated on designating ourselves a role. In his lecture, *Existentialism and Humanism* Sartre states "being precedes essence" meaning we are not the specific things we hope for but rather an infinite possibility of things that we must let our experience and being determine. We must understand growth comes from adjusting to what is and not what could be.

The caged bird sings
with a fearful trill
of things unknown
but longed for still
and his tune is heard
on the distant hill
for the caged bird
sings of freedom. – Maya Angelou

Our aversion to unfamiliar and inconvenient conditions forges the iron of the shackles that perpetuate our bondage. Growth is a product of deficiency. However, we are taught growth is becoming the best at a single activity. If a person obtains a senior title after thirty years of working for a company, where have they grown? What success have they gained aside from neglecting their capacity to be a multi-faceted being? Music artist Lauryn Hill refers to life as being a cycle of learning and mastership or a sequence of peaks and valleys. At times, we reach a summit in which we have mastered a subject. Once we reach this level we should embrace redirection. We should embrace leaving the top of one hill and being afoot another hill. Growth can only be achieved by propelling a wrecking ball toward everything we think we know and using what we learned to build on the little that we do know.

Chapter Twenty: On Fame

"Fame is the worst drug known to man. It's stronger than, heroin. When you could look in the mirror like, "There I am" and still not see, what you've become"
- Jay-z (Shawn Carter)

The idea of fame is often associated with celebrity stardom. However, this is merely the most extreme form of the notion. At some point in our lives we will be inclusive to the dynamic that perpetuates the general concept. The idea of fame is present in any community or organization in which its inhibitors are in constant contact; this continual interaction creates a system that induces us to categorize each other. Think about the dynamic of small towns, religious institutions, or colleges. The restricted nature of places like this force us to focus on people and events. They are reference points for discussions and entertainment. Once we are no longer in these settings the same people and events lose their importance. If we were to start a conversation about them in a new setting it would be met with little enthusiasm.

For a celebrity, the entire world is this community and these dynamics exist on a higher scale.

Still, regardless of the level, fame requires an abundance of short term sacrifices and grants no long-term benefit.

There are many underlining reasons why we yearn to be famous but in a sentence – We pursue fame because of our insecurities. We want to prove our worth to specific people by being deemed as important by the world. But, fame is the epitome of Pandora's Box. It encompasses a seemingly great reward but results in more complicated problems than it solves. Fame requires us to wear masks. These masks exhibit the favorable traits we possess, the traits that the world admires about us. Unfortunately, in the process of wearing these masks the world forgets we are more than any one mask. Once we remove these masks we are met with scorn and criticism and are forced to quickly put them back on. We eventually become so used to wearing these masks we forget we have them on.

Fame entails an incomparable amount of self-sacrifice. The effort required to prove ourselves to this larger audience becomes greater than the energy needed to prove ourselves to the initial group. The more we divulge about ourselves to the public to receive praise, the more we open ourselves to criticism, and hence we become guarded and isolated. This evokes a feeling of loneliness even when we are the focal point of millions of people.

Still, receiving this level of praise is addictive. It instills within the person an excessive sense of self-worth. If not consciously monitored it transcends into conceit. The idea that people need us is empowering. When the number of people who depend on us becomes too large it agitates the ego. It incites an unappreciative response. It disconnects us from reality as we become more of a symbol than a relatable human being. Attention from this many people makes it an arduous task to distinguish genuine care from infatuation. Consequently, the people who suffer the most from our acquisition of fame are usually the people who cared about us prior to us obtaining it.

One of the most destructive effects of fame is it conjures incremental changes that result in something worse than the loss of our identity - the development of a new one. The person in the mirror physically looks the same but inside at their core they have changed drastically. Fame discards the things that make us, us. The person that remains is one that is not a captive of limited resources. Money, attention, and assurance are in abundance; this is a price the soul pays. The people who are now attracted to us come with an asterisk. Among many things, the acquisition of fame forfeits our entitlement to privacy. Which to some extent forfeits our tranquility. We become public proprietary.

The demand for us to be pleasing becomes unremitting. We ignore the few consequences we do acknowledge because we believe fame will grant us a permanent place in history. Marcus Aurelius offers

insight on this idea in his writing *Meditations*. He states"
He who has a powerful desire for posthumous fame does
not consider that every one of those who remember him
will himself also die very soon; then again also they who
have succeeded them, until the whole remembrance shall
have been extinguished as it is transmitted through men
who foolishly admire and then perish. But suppose that
those who will remember are even immortal, and that the
remembrance will be immortal, what good will this do
you?" Aurelius is excavating an idea that few people
consider when pursuing the approval of others. One day
we all die. Therefore, the opinion of people is of little
importance. Aurelius references death to illustrate this
idea, but the concept can be seen at any point when we
leave our closed communities, institutions or
organizations.

The typical high school class clown is a good
example of this. He pursues fame or the approval of his
classmates by performing jokes during class. In exchange
for his entertainment he receives acknowledgement and
popularity. Both are satisfying in the moment. But the
consequence of his jokes will be reflected in his grades
and his inability to receive references from his teachers.
He ignores this because he has no reference point.
Currently, high school is his peak and hence seems never
ending. He believes his antics will be etched in the minds
of his classmates forever. He gives little thought to the
idea that once this group graduates his sacrifices will be

in vain. In a sense their opinions of him die or lose all value once high school ends. This being the case it is pointless for him to ever pursue it.

Pursuing fame on any level entails the same tradeoff - sacrificing the stability of tomorrow for the temporary pleasures of today.

Chapter Twenty-One: On Absence & Misfortune

"So remember this principle when something threatens to cause you pain: the thing itself was no misfortune at all; to endure it and prevail is great good fortune."
- Marcus Aurelius

Seldom do we attach a positive connotation to the idea of absence. We view blessings in the form of having or receiving. But the absence of something can be equally if not more rewarding than its presence. When things are removed from our life they grant us the opportunity for progression. Like a snake shedding its skin, within this window of absence we grow. When we hold onto pieces of our lives due to contentment, they become stifling – i.e.) If we lose our job we view it as the loss of something valuable, instead of an opportunity. Without changes that induce absence, there are substantial components of our lives that remain fixed. Vacancy is a gift. Openings in our life hold the possibility for something greater, something different.

We look at life from an inside out perspective. We avoid absence because we dislike the idea there is now a closed door we must find our way through. But remember from the outside in, your life now contains an open door. One that was fortified with chains and locks. We should constantly remind ourselves closed hands can't receive. Absence is sometimes a present. It awakens the wanderer within us. Without it we may never set sail on the voyages intended to fill the vacancy. President Barack Obama's story is an exceptional example. The absence of his father was an essential part of his journey. In his book, *Dreams from my Father* the President explains the impact this absence had on him. If his father was present, he may have never gained the ambition to pursue the presidency.

Absence is one of the many misfortunes we should learn to appreciate. Misfortune is not evil; it is a necessity. Occasional instances of peril allow us to discover ourselves. Hardship is the instrument which sharpens us. It is the guiding light that leads us to our purpose. What is misfortune but challenges that allow us to develop and test our strength? Ancient Greek philosopher Epictetus elaborates on this idea in his writing *The Discourses*. He states "What do you think that Hercules would have been if there had not been such a lion, and hydra, and stag, and boar, and certain unjust and bestial men, whom Hercules used to drive away and clear out? And what would he have been doing if there had been nothing of the kind?" Epictetus's questions are enlightening.

Adversity is not an easy part of life, but it is an essential piece of it. We become so engulfed by our unfortunate circumstances we don't realize they reveal just how much power we possess. They force us to dig deep into parts of us, parts we did not know exist. If not for misfortune how could we be anything more than the feeble and unpolished creatures, we were birthed into this world as.

Yes, our lives are full of unexplainable destruction, tragedy, and pain, but on the other side of it all is evolution. Like Hercules, like Obama, and like so many others, misfortune creates our story. Imagine the alternative. A life in which everything went as we expected. Imagine we could learn how to ride a bike without falling. An appealing thought at first. But what do you remember about your first attempt at this task? Take away the adversity and it is an unmemorable moment. The process of learning how to ride your bike was defined by consistently falling, and one day having the power, the knowledge to keep going. What joy or experiences could be obtained without misfortune? It takes awareness and maturity to realize misfortune makes life special. There is purpose in everything, it is the rare moments when that purpose is revealed which is the true blessing. Although our battles aren't with mythical creatures, we display our capacity to be superheroes by fighting them.

If progression is the ultimate result of misfortunate, why is it deemed negative? The answer is entitlement. We feel entitled to control and order. We believe we are in full control of our life and when something compromises this we meet it with resentment. But if we take away our self-interested position in these events, we view them with sympathy but also rationality. This is the reason we can watch events happen to others and approach it with an understanding but detached response. We can console, give advice and even point out the lessons that may be learned because there is no personal attachment.

The Ancient Greeks were notorious for their use of tragedy and misfortune in theater. So much so Plato and Aristotle developed theories on how it should most effectively be implemented in plays. The unfavorable perception of misfortune is a result of a battle between the mind's idea of reality and reality itself. German philosopher Hegel explains this in his writing *Aesthetics: Lectures on Fine Art*. He states "The original essence of tragedy consists then in the fact that within such a conflict each of the opposed sides, if taken by itself, has justification, while on the other hand each can establish the true and positive content of its own aim and character only by negating and damaging the equally justified power of the other." We believe undesirable outcomes are unjust. Reality poses a conflicting idea. We must accept reality is not what should happen but what does happen.

Once we internalize this, we can redirect our attention away from questioning why the event happened and focus on the growth that may come from it. We must understand we are not the center of the universe. In his writing *On the Shortness of Life* Seneca states "What can happen to one can happen to all." If you let this idea sink into your vitals, and regard all the ills of other people as having a clear path to you too, you will be armed long before you are attacked. It is too late for the mind to equip itself to endure dangers once they are already there." The Stoic Philosopher is arguing we make misfortune our enemy. We are too selfish and narrow-minded to view misfortunate as an unpaved road. We don't take time to witness the cars ahead of us and around us who are also hitting the potholes and speedbumps.

In the same work, Seneca states "Some are restricted to one place by exile, others by priesthoods: all life is a servitude. So you have to get used to your circumstances, complain about them as little as possible, and grasp whatever advantage they have to offer." Alternatively put, misfortune is a powerful tool, only we decide what role it has in our lives.

Chapter Twenty-Two: On Choice & Probability

"You may think that in life, a lot of things happen to you along the way. The truth is, in life, you happen to a lot of things."
- Shad Helmstetter

Every choice we make connects and leads to another choice. In the simplest definition, life is merely a series of choices. Therefore, our decisions are the single most impactful factor in determining the course of our lives. We can split our choices into two categories I) Choices based on probability II) Choices based on mindful causality. The first group encompasses choices we unconsciously make and are often based on chance. Think about where and how you met the most important people in your life. The decision to skip a party, take a different route home, or not to start a conversation had the potential to drastically change your life. The second group encompasses choices we are aware will have significant implications on our lives. Decisions such as which subject you want to study in college, who you want to marry, or whether to commit a crime can be placed in this group. We begin to make choices that are most conducive to our happiness and well-being when we realize the choices made in both groups derive from our deposition.

At every reaction point, there are an infinite number of ways we can choose to respond. Because we have so many choices we counter-intuitively only have one. If you were told to choose 1 cup out of 1,000 cups, the cup you chose would carry a special sentiment to you. The improbability that you chose that specific cup is more aligned with your disposition than chance. It is more likely you picked the cup from the top left corner because you traditionally feel this section is a lucky area or you chose a green cup because you have an affinity for the color. The choices we make every day are guided by the same logic. Our choices are a result of our deposition. The more efficient we become at integrating good habits into our disposition the more we enable our unconscious decisions to be equally as beneficial as our conscious ones.

Our character is exhibited in our choices. By adjusting our character, we adjust our decisions. Seneca advocates for this idea in his writing *Letters from a Stoic*. He states "How much better to pursue a straight course and eventually reach that destination where the things that are pleasant and the things that are honourable finally become for you, the same." Seneca is implying we should practice making the choices that are pleasurable to us and the choices that are most beneficial to our well-being the same. Once we accomplish this, we will begin to habitually make choices that are both enjoyable and in are best interest. For example, exercising. The more we exercise and attach a favorable connotation to the action, the more it becomes a habitual and unconscious choice. After a while it will feel irregular or upsetting for us not to exercise. We will feel uncomfortable not partaking in this action. The decision to not exercise will feel as if we are dishonoring ourselves. At this point the choice that brings us happiness is the same that is in our best-interest. The same could be said about how we view eating well, learning, or what qualities we deem are important in a significant other. If we wish to become outspoken, we should force ourselves to regularly speak in uncomfortable situations. We should do this until the point we feel cowardly for not sharing our thoughts. If we wish to become more social, we should force ourselves to go to social events, until we feel oddly bored at home. The better we become at this task, the more confident we can be in our decision making when it is on auto-pilot.

When we internalize the idea that we are responsible for our own lives, we take a critical step in our development. We are responsible for both our conscious and unconscious decisions. It is our responsibility to be the person we want. French Philosopher J.P. Sartre believed having so many options to choose from has made us fearful of our freedom of choice. We are afraid of making the wrong one. Consequently, we let others dictate what we want to be. He offers advice on the importance of choices in his lecture *Existentialism Is a Humanism*. He states, "In life, a man commits himself, draws his own portrait, and there is nothing but that portrait." Sartre is insinuating our life and the choices it entails must come from us. If they do not our life or the portrait of it loses meaning to the only critic that matters, the painter.

We are taught we should make smart choices. The problem is smart choices are defined as safe choices. The two are not interchangeable. Adjusting our disposition to be inclusive of the traits conducive to becoming the person we want to be is the only way to make smart choices. At times this means making the most unsafe and terrifying choice. However, these choices inevitably catapult us into the most fulfilling life possible.

Chapter Twenty-Three: On Idolatry

"The moment you doubt whether you can fly, you cease forever to be able to do it."
- J.M. Barrie

A distinction must be made between role models and idols. Role models serve as influential figures. We aspire to possess their talents, character, and achievements. We admire their contributions and hope to one day emulate them. Contrarily, we worship idols. We praise their attributes and gifts and wish we were of similar magnitude. The underlining difference is the intent to emulate vs. the intent to worship. Idolization has a disruptive impact on how we interpret and utilize our capacity. When we idolize others, we undermine the idea we possess an equivalent capacity. We ignore the idea we have the same time and potential to be an equal or better version of that person. We place these individuals on an unreachable pedestal and in doing so we mitigate our own abilities. The time exhausted admiring these figures could be placed in harvesting our own talents.

Idolization occurs when admiration transcends from personal aspirations to acts of veneration. This is an unwarranted transition. In his writing, *Meditations,* Marcus Aurelius states "Everything which is beautiful is beautiful in itself, and it is sufficient in itself, not needing praise for itself." The Stoic Emperor is describing the futility of earthly praise. The talents, charisma, and character of others are inherent features. They are behaviors that everyone can cultivate in some form for themselves. They deserve adoration, not displays of praise. Nothing is gained by the creation of fan pages, sculptures, and similar exhibitions. When we hang up posters of people like we do art, we liken them to abstract figures. Subconsciously we place their capabilities outside of human boundaries.

This is most detrimental to admirers who do not share common aspirations as their idol. In this case the admirer has decided to live vicariously through their idol. To some extent the admirer believes they share the success of their idol, despite them being separate beings. Epictetus elaborates on this idea in his writing *The Enchiridion*. He states "Don't be prideful with any excellence that is not your own. If a horse should be prideful and say, "I am handsome," it would be supportable. But when you are prideful, and say, " I have a handsome horse," know that you are proud of what is, in fact, only the good of the horse. What, then, is your own? Only your reaction to the appearances of things. Thus, when you behave conformably to nature in reaction to how things appear, you will be proud with reason; for you will take pride in some good of your own." Epictetus is arguing the talents of others belong to their possessor, therefore outsiders should not extract pride from them.

Instead of meeting figures of aspiration with excessive adoration, it is more advantageous to convey the opposite sentiment – competition. Psychologist Edward Tory Higgin's "Self-Discrepancy Theory" argues we have several different senses of our being, our actual selves and ideal selves being two of them. Our desire to synchronize these selves motivates us to change. We should view figures of aspiration as our ideal selves. Consequently, we should make them our rivals. We should use them as benchmarks. We should challenge ourselves to reach or surpass their status – as opposed to being simply enthralled by them.

Chapter Twenty-Four: On Ego & Humility

"I and me are always too deeply in conversation"
- Friedrich Nietzsche

Wars are most often won by rulers who have little ego or many allies. The ego can be destructive, yet it provides instinctual guidance. In a pessimistic world, there are times our ego will be the only support we have. Pride is its language. Our ego helps us determine our self-worth, and capabilities. Consequently, we should not deem the presence of the ego as negative but rather exercise its use with caution and solely as a last resort. Our ego essentially helps us undermine the expectations of others, in doing so we create personal expectations that can be equally as disadvantageous. If not properly monitored these personal expectations can become blinding. They compel us to become so focused on how significant we are we stop seeing the entire picture. This encapsulates the ego's greatest weakness – constraint.

To survive the ego must extract from negative emotions such as hate, vanity, narcissism and jealousy. In the process the ego creates enemies and repels those who's intentions maybe to help us. Our egos will always restrict how flexible we are in our interactions. As a result, the ego is a luxury only a man with many friends and connections can afford.

Seldom do we consider the valuable properties of the less explored absence of the ego. When we release our ego, we become limitless. Not only do we silence the expectations of others, we silence our own expectations. In doing so we are able to simply perform, without the fear of failure. Discarding our ego enables us to focus on the destination rather than the path. We become unafraid to be the initiator of actions that are conducive to the final goal. We obtain a bird's eye view of each situation and hence we gain the willingness and wisdom to make necessary sacrifices. There is power in the unbiased, impersonal, and impartial element of objective judgment. This entails the strength of the absence of the ego. The Philosopher King Marcus Aurelius supports this idea in his writing *Meditations*. He states "Objective judgement, now, at this very moment. Unselfish action, now, at this very moment. Willing acceptance – now, at this very moment – of all external events. That's all you need." Aurelius understood objective judgement expands our options, makes us resourceful and places us in a greater position to succeed. The ego offers pride but the lack of one offers an even greater gift - versatility.

Among the greatest assets of concealing the ego is its ability to influence our tenacity. When the ego experiences failure it must dig deeper into the negative sentiments that perpetuate it. It must hate a little more to continue; It must envy a little harder to carry on. Without the ego, there is nothing for failure to hurt. This enables us to embody Winston Churchills definition of success - going from failure to failure without loss of enthusiasm. The lack of the ego incites modesty. When we lack a sense of entitlement for victory, we work harder to obtain it.

Humility is knowing no matter how great your accomplishments or how low your defeats, there are people with so much less than you they may never know either. Our worries are an extension of our perception of the world. When we become grateful for everything we have and make seeing the good in people and situations a habit we unlock the power to succeed not merely for ourselves but also in a way that benefits others. To contribute anything worth producing we must have humility. This meekness is only attainable through the disposal of the ego. When humility is not present our inventions are unsubstantial, damaging, and an unneeded addition to humanity.

The ego is alluring. We seek refuge in its familiarity when enduring difficult times. However, the ego comes with a price that we often ignore. We lose important pieces of ourselves when we lean on its abilities. We jeopardize significant people and inventions by pursuing its benefits. Therefore, it's imperative we learn how to identify instances when it is of greater value to suppress it. The ego is initiated in instances when there is internal resistance to external thought. Three chambers of inconsonance – (1) emotional imbalance, (2) self-righteousness, and (3) forbearance define the process of its emergence and the key to defusing its presence.

The first glimpse of the ego is captured when we encounter ideas that challenge our own beliefs. This occurrence provokes emotions of inferiority, and unworthiness. The ego is our first line of defense to offset and defend the emotional imbalance that we are being subjected to. Hence, the first and most effective way to disengage the ego is by building our emotional intelligence. Once we are able to identify why our ego is arising we develop the tools needed to impede it before the damage is done. When we learn how to control our emotions we learn how to use the ego constructively. If the emotional imbalance isn't contained at this preliminary point, a need for alignment is signaled. Once this justification is made, the ego acts on sentiments of self-righteousness, becoming infatuated with proving itself as correct. In an effort to protect and repair, its actions are directed to belittle, demean, and disregard its provoker. Its only concern is preserving its own identity. It is not so much the ego's goal that is dangerous but its means in achieving it. The ego works on isolated thought, attacking the ideas of others. It feeds off disproving and its greatest reward is the feeling of being right, even if this feeling is merely an illusion. In doing so, it abandons the idea that we can simultaneously protect our own thoughts, and respect the thoughts of others - furthermore it is unseeing to the idea that sometimes the greater victory is allowing someone else's ideas to be the prevailing thought even if it is not the absolute truth. Hence, introducing the last chamber – forbearance. To rescind the ego, we need to internalize the idea that being right does not equate to being justice-bearing. When the conquest to being right is clouded by feelings of inferiority it is simply being self-serving. We create an overinflated image of ourselves that debilitates us from having a meaningful impact on humanity. When we lessen the ego, we expand our influence.

Chapter Twenty-Five: On Introverts

"One life is all we have and we live it as we believe in living it. But to sacrifice what you are and to live without belief, that is a fate more terrible than dying."
- Joan of Arc

To enjoy a fulfilling life, we must live in accordance with our own nature and inclinations. We must be willing to discover who we are, and more importantly accept the person we find. If we do not, we will eventually realize the rewards and superlatives enjoyed by others bring us little joy. The introvert serves as an exceptional example. The interests and inclinations of introverts diverge greatly from what is normally accepted. Extroversion is the quintessential standard in which society is mounted upon. It is applauded in professional, academic, and institutional environments. As a result, introverts are misunderstood and spend a considerable amount of their lives in some form trying to assimilate to an extrovert favored culture.

Introverts prefer to interact with people they are comfortable with. They prefer to invest all their time and energy on these select individuals. The more social interaction an introvert engages in with people outside their sphere of comfort, the less fulfilled they feel. Because of this, most people deem introverts as anti-social, when in fact they are merely selective. They favor activities structured around solitude and prefer to skip the social activities that many people find enjoyable such as parties and concerts. Hence, a common misconception is introverts experience lives that are less fun than others. This is only because the generally accepted definition of fun is being projected upon introverts. For introverts, there is a substantial difference in being by themselves and being alone. An introvert is essentially their own best friend. This is incomprehensible to many people but this trait allows introverts to have a great relationship and understanding of themselves. It enables them to obtain a level of peace and comfort many people yearn to experience.

Essentially one individual may see happiness, normalness, and achievement in a very different light than another. Philosopher Friedrich Nietzsche offers his assistance on this manner in his essay *Schopenhauer as Educator*. He states "No one can build you the bridge on which you, and only you, must cross the river of life. There may be countless trails and bridges and demigods who would gladly carry you across; but only at the price of pawning and forgoing yourself. There is one path in the world that none can walk but you. Where does it lead? Don't ask, walk!" Nietzsche is arguing the lifestyles we pursue brings us satisfaction on a case by case basis. An aspiring painter has a different perception of success than an aspiring businessman. Even if the painter were to become successful by assimilating to the image of happiness of the businessman, the painter himself would be unfulfilled.

In the end, the path to a fulfilling life is through knowledge of self. Still, obtaining this knowledge is one of the most challenging tasks in our journey through life. In the same essay, Philosopher Friedrich Nietzsche shares his ideas on the importance of self-awareness. He states "How can man know himself? It is a dark, mysterious business: if a hare has seven skins, a man may skin himself seventy times seven times without being able to say, "Now that is truly you; that is no longer your outside." It is also an agonizing, hazardous undertaking thus to dig into oneself, to climb down toughly and directly into the tunnels of one's being... Let the young soul survey its own life with a view of the following question: "What have you truly loved thus far? What has ever uplifted your soul, what has dominated and delighted it at the same time?" Assemble these revered objects in a row before you and perhaps they will reveal a law by their nature and their order: the fundamental law of your very self." The assessment Nietzsche proposes is not one that is foreign to us. We naturally conduct this self-assessment to guide ourselves back to the correct path. The problem is not formulating the answers to these questions, but accepting them.

Furthermore, accepting we possess the ability to make the needed adjustments that coincide with them. We often have strong aversions toward pliable aspects of our lives, but we continue to engage in these actions because they tend to the nature of our ideal selves. We hate cold places yet we continue to live in cold cities. Scenarios like this are more adjustable than we like to admit. We find reasons to justify why they can't be changed, instead of developing ways to make the change happen. The next time you analyze yourself, use Nietzsche's proposed questions, answer them and do not debate your initial answers. Make it a habit to ask yourself, if no one was watching how much joy would I extract from this person, action, or activity. That person is who you are.

If we told a sheep the attributes it needed to mimic to be seen as a wolf how valuable would this information be? Although it would be praised by others, how happy could this sheep become by emulating something it is not, something it in fact despises. No matter how well it learned to run, jump or hunt; it is still inherently a sheep. When you find out who you are, believe it. Introverts are handed a world that is upside down. However, it is only when they attempt to rationalize their nature and inclinations according to others that they lose the ability to have an enjoyable life.

Introverts are just one example; the principle is applicable to any group of outsiders.

Chapter Twenty-Six: On Honesty & Transparency

"History will absolve me."
- Fidel Castro

We lie not because we are afraid to meet the expectations of others, but rather the expectations of ourselves. It is our fear of inadequacy that prevents us from being truthful. When we lie, we are merely projecting our insecurities into the world. Therefore, the truth is less about servicing others, but conquering ourselves. The truth encompasses two enticing attributes I) It presents the opportunity for correction II) It's constant, which allows it to conjure the same impact heedless of when it surfaces. Still, we find contentment in our lies. We receive satisfaction from them in the same way we do by avoiding doctor visits. When we lie, we neglect the universe's corrective nature. i.e.) - When our boss asks if we feel overwhelmed by our workload or our teacher asks if we need help with the coursework, even if we are in need of assistance, our natural instinct is to convey we are in control. We are uncertain of our abilities. We fear if we admit the truth, we will look incapable. Consider the alternative. When we admit to ourselves that we need help and find the confidence to confess the truth, the path to correction is presented to us. Our boss provides us with more resources. Our teacher provides us with a tutor. In all cases, when we lie we deprive ourselves of these necessary opportunities for correction. Nonetheless, the inevitable corrective action will take place by less than desirable means.

The effects of truthfulness are universal. They are pertinent regardless if we are confessing to infidelity, acknowledging our faults, or exposing corruption. However, more than our personal development is at stake in cases involving the latter. When we are not lobbyist for the truth regarding social issues we rob society of the needed corrective measures. In other words, telling the truth is a duty. It is an obligation that we owe to society. German Philosopher Immanuel Kant defends this idea in his essay *On the Supposed Right to Lie from Benevolent Motives*. He states "To be truthful in all declarations is therefore a sacred command of reason prescribing unconditionally, one not to be restricted by any conveniences." Kant is removing altruism and all other conditions as justified means to lie. He is alluding to the question regarding truthfulness that we find most challenging - is the concept of duty separable from the concept of right? Simply put, is it ok to lie sometimes? Kant uses this question to introduce a scenario commonly referred to as "Lying to the Murderer at the Door." Kant states if a murderer arrived at our door and asks for the location of his next victim (who is inside our house) we are obligated to tell the truth and disclose this information.

Kant's argument was and continues to be a source of controversy. In the same essay, he defends his position in the following: "if you have kept strictly to the truth, then public justice can hold nothing against you, whatever the unforeseen consequences might be. It is still possible that, after you have honestly answered "yes" to the murderer's question as to whether his enemy is at home, the latter has nevertheless gone out unnoticed, so that he would not meet the murderer and the deed would not be done; but if you had lied and said that he is not at home, and he has actually gone out (though you are not aware of it), so that the murderer encounters him while going away and perpetrates his deed on him, then you can by right be prosecuted as the author of his death. For if you had told the truth to the best of your knowledge, then neighbors might have come and apprehended the murderer while he was searching the house for his enemy and the deed would have been prevented." Kant is arguing that when we lie with the intention to help others, the truth does not simply cease to exist. By lying to the murderer in Kant's example, the potential victim is only safe for the time being. It is this feeling of being safe in the moment that makes us content with our lies. In the process, we are forfeiting our ability to create sustainable solutions to situations. The murderer does not simply go home after asking the location of his victim and disclosing his intentions. The lie (the potential victim is not home) did not change the situation. It simply delayed it. The murderer has the opportunity to plan and try again.

We must embrace the idea that situations don't get better from the absence of truth. They are merely cloaked until they reach an inevitable boiling point. This is evident on a societal level - revolutions form from oppression, volatile weather from climate change. Although a challenging task we must find the means to stand for truth or prepare to endure the inescapable consequences.

Truthfulness is a difficult pursuit for two reasons. I) It requires an unfamiliar level of transparency. We've become accustom to shutting down when we are unable or afraid to express ourselves. This is the most convenient option. The idea of being bare and fully visible to the world is intimidating. It requires effort and courage but it is advantageous. Transparency can alleviate some of our burdens. It allows us to spread the battles we are trying to fight alone. It explicitly indicates to the world what we want and it gives the world the opportunity to help us obtain it.

Humanity has been given many great abilities. Mindreading is not one. Until we explore the upside of transparency we will continually receive uninvited responses. II) It destroys people's perception of reality. Consequently, the truth is often unwelcomed. Lauryn

Hill summarizes this concept in an interview stating "Whenever you stand for something and you stand for goodness or truth you will always get resistance ... whenever you stand for truth and the service of others." Hill is alluding to the idea that for some people a false reality is an advantageous reality. So much so they will challenge and attempt to dismantle any threat to it. As difficult as the pursuit of truthfulness maybe, it remains a worthy journey. Telling the truth offers varied results, results that are sometimes displeasing to others and even to ourselves. Nonetheless, no matter how costly it seems, truthfulness is the only path that offers the needed results. Francis Bacon reiterates this idea in his essay *On Truth*. He states "Truth may perhaps come to the price of a pearl, that showeth best by day; but it will not rise to the price of a diamond or carbuncle, that showeth best in varied lights." Bacon is conveying the idea that although the truth may seem costlier than a lie, in due time it will prove its value.

The special thing about transparency is it allows light not only to come from us but also through us. It allows light in. Truthfulness is often not rewarded overnight. It takes time and patience. When it does bear gifts, they are altruistic and fruitful. In an interview, President Obama captures this idea while reflecting on his legacy as president. He states "If my voice has been true and positive, then my hope would be that it may not fix everything right away ... that's OK. We plant seeds, and somebody else maybe sits under the shade of the tree that we planted … and I'd like to think that, as best as I could, I have been true in speaking about these issues." He is hopeful, as we all should be when we confide in the truth, that one day history will absolve us.

Chapter Twenty-Seven: On Death

Life for me ain't been no crystal stair.
It's had tacks in it,
And splinters,
And boards torn up,
And places with no carpet on the floor
Bare.
But all the time
I'se been a-climbin' on
- Excerpt from Langston Hughes poem *Mother to Son*

     The idea of death should be revered for the same reason we admire panoramic views of a city, the sight of oceans, the view of waterfalls, or the magnitude of mountains. They make us feel small. Death is a constant reminder that regardless of our social or economic status we are no more or less important than any other human being. It is the one indisputable constant that commands we are equal. Death incites feelings of vulnerability and insufficiency. These feelings intensify our desire to achieve substantial things. If life was endless we would lack such motivation.

     Our fear of death is not contrived from our discontentment with the limited time we possess but a resentment towards the restrictions placed on what we are able to do with this time. Marcus Aurelius puts this idea in context in his writing *Meditations*. He states "Thou mayest foresee also the things which will be. For they will certainly be of like form, and it is not possible that they should deviate from the order of the things which take place now; accordingly, to have contemplated human life for forty years is the same as to have contemplated it for ten thousand years. For what more wilt thou see?" The Philosopher King is arguing that life is merely a reoccurring sequence of events and themes that are occasionally occupied with new faces and objects. He is arguing that in forty years a man has experienced all that life has to offer. What more can he see in ten thousand years that he has not already seen in this time?

This being the case. It's how we spend our time here that makes us begrudge death. We are aware that we are being cheated out of this limited time and consequently we resent leaving. If we go on a vacation with friends – when the trip is fun and satisfying, we are more than willing to leave. We feel like we have enjoyed our time there and are ready to return home or set out on the next adventure. Compare this to going on a trip with a friend who forces us to do activities we are uninterested in. We feel unfulfilled and dread the idea we have squandered our time at this place. Ultimately, we fear death because we do not live life how we want. In doing so we fail to create a legacy for ourselves that we are comfortable leaving.

We all have a story. We have an unwavering desire to share the views and perceptions that we have gained through our experiences. Yet, societal pressures suppress our ability to create. Hence, we fear that we will be forgotten and our time here was in vein. The more we are able to create and leave extensions of ourselves, the less frightening the idea of death becomes.

We do not understand death; therefore, it is natural for us to fear it. Still, what we can cherish about death is its ability to help us appreciate life. German Philosopher Martin Heidegger argued that we often forget that we are alive because we are consumed by our day to day activities. It is only in the few moments when we are alone or in contact with nature that we acknowledge our existence. These moments combat the egotism that plagues our daily lives. It helps us view the world with a widened perspective. Death is among the greatest stimulators of this feeling. It forces us to reach an unfamiliar and alarming epiphany. That we are but a single piece in a complicated puzzle. Yet, once we reach this epiphany we are able to step away from the question of "how is my piece the solution to this puzzle?" and focus on how we can influence and affect the other pieces. In an interview, Heidegger was asked how we can we better lead our lives he responded by saying "We

should simply aim to spend more times in graveyards."
Death reminds us how we should aspire to live.

No matter if you feel happy, sad, angry, or depressed - you feel... therefore you are alive. Society fills our minds with insecurities. Consequently, we spend our entire lives focusing on what we lack instead of what we have. Think about a celebrity that you admire who lost their life at a young age. Think about all the things they possessed that you do not. Still, if you are reading this at this moment you own something of great value, your life. This is a treasure they would surely tell you is of far greater significance than any gift the world can grant us.

Step away from this book for one minute and imagine right now at this moment you were to die.

As you are leaving your body, ask yourself what do you wish you had done more? What do you wish you had done less? Who do you wish you had told you loved? Who do you wish you had treated better? Now come back to reality and make your answers come true... because you can.

Life makes us focus on how important we look to others. Death makes us focus on how important we are to others. The idea of death mitigates the stressful and daunting challenges in our lives that are in fact - trivial.

It magnifies aspects of our lives that we take for granted. So, being afraid to die is ok. It's being afraid to live, that is unacceptable.

Seldom do we step back and truly analyze our own importance relative to others. When we do, we realize, from our perspective we are stuck in traffic, but to the people in the cars aside and behind us we are the traffic. Death helps us realize there is no traffic jam.

"So, now at last we've come to this great problem, this question. The problem of mutual understanding. How can blind and sighted people truly understand each other? How can men understand women? How can the rich understand the poor? How can the old understand the young? Can we have insights into other people? This is the great question upon which the unity of humanity hangs." - John Hull

"When we ask this question we quickly find a substantial answer. We see how deeply a crack can run through one's flowerpot." - Troy Drayton

Afterword

Thank you for taking the time to read this story. When I began creating this project, I never imagined it would have the reach it has today. With its completion, I feel blessed and fortunate to have had the opportunity to make one of my dreams come true. I hope the words resonated with you and inspire new thoughts, happiness, and an internal sense of wholeness.

Stay connected with us on Instagram for more insightful and thought provoking content:
@thecobblestoneflowerpot

& stop by our Amazon page to leave a review!

Made in the USA
San Bernardino, CA
28 December 2018